live theatre

CW00494455

Iris

By Alison Carr

***Iris* is a Live Theatre production and had its world premiere at Live Theatre, Newcastle on Thursday 7th April 2016.**
It was performed from Wednesday 6 to Saturday 30 April 2016.

The original cast were Katy Cavanagh, Joe Caffrey and Sam Neale.

The production was supported by the Friends of Live Theatre

SERVING THEATRE SF SINCE 1830

WWW.SAMUELFRENCH.CO.UK
WWW.SAMUELFRENCH.COM

CAST

Julie	Katy Cavanagh
Ruby	Sam Neale
Gerry	Joe Caffrey

CREATIVE & PRODUCTION TEAM

Writer	Alison Carr
Director	Max Roberts
Designer	Patrick Connellan
Lighting Design	Drummond Orr
Sound Design	Dave Flynn
Production Manager	Drummond Orr
Creative Producer	Graeme Thompson
Stage Manager	Adam Johnston
Deputy Stage Manager	Heather Robertson
Technical Manager	Dave Flynn
Technician	Craig Spence
Costume Supervisor	Lou Duffy
Professional Casting	Lucy Jenkins CDG & Sooki McShane CDG
Prop Maker	Paul Aziz

Thanks
Chris Auld, photography, Cathy Gillespie, design and Ian McLaughlin, filming

live theatre

Live Theatre is recognised as one of the great new writing producing theatres on the international stage and is deeply rooted in Newcastle and Gateshead where we are based.

We believe that creativity and cultural engagement are central to the lives of individuals and arts and culture should be recognised, supported and celebrated as significant contributors to the creative and economic wellbeing of our communities.

As well as championing the art of writing for the stage by producing and presenting new plays, Live Theatre unlocks the potential of young people and finds and nurtures creative talent. It also leads and demonstrates future thinking on new models of business sustainability and growth.

Founded in 1973, the theatre was transformed in 2007 with a capital redevelopment. The result is a beautifully restored and refurbished complex of five Grade II listed buildings with state-of-the-art facilities in a unique historical setting, including a 160-seat cabaret-style theatre, a studio theatre, renovated rehearsal rooms, a series of dedicated writers' rooms as well as a thriving café, bar and pub.

Live Theatre is a national leader in developing new strategies for increasing income and assets for the charity. In 2016 the company is completing Live Works, a £10 million capital development of quayside-fronted land and buildings adjacent to the theatre, to create a children's and young people's writing centre, a public park and a new commercial office space.

Live Works joins award-winning pub The Broad Chare, online course www.beaplaywright.com and The Schoolhouse (an office space for SMEs), as one of Live Theatre's creative enterprises, which increases funds through new income streams.

For more information see **www.live.org.uk**

Live Theatre is grateful for the support of Arts Council England and Newcastle City Council as well as its many other supporters and friends

ARTS COUNCIL ENGLAND

Supported using public funding by
ARTS COUNCIL ENGLAND

Community Foundation
Newcastle Culture Investment Fund
Supported by Newcastle City Council

STAFF AT LIVE THEATRE

Chief Executive Jim Beirne
Artistic Director Max Roberts
Operations Director Wendy Barnfather
Administrator to the Director Clare Gowens

Finance, Events & Venue Hire
Finance Manager Antony Robertson
Finance Officer Catherine Moody
Finance Assistant Helen Tuffnell
Events & Venue Hire Administrator Chris Foley

Marketing
Marketing Manager Cait Read
Marketing Manager (Maternity Leave) Claire Cockroft
Marketing & Press Officer Lisa Campbell
Marketing & Press Officer Melanie Rashbrooke
Box Office Administrator Amy Foley

Development
Director of Enterprise & Development Lucy Bird
Development Manager Lizzy Skingley

Education & Participation
Director of Education & Engagement Helen Moore
Associate Director Paul James
Resident Drama Worker Jon Luke McKie
Resident Drama Worker Toni McElhatton
Resident Drama Worker Christina Castling
Administrator Roisin Crowley Linton

Literary
Literary Manager Gez Casey
Creative Producer Graeme Thompson
Administrator Degna Stone

Production & Technical
Production Manager Drummond Orr
Technical Manager Dave Flynn
Technician Craig Spence

House Management
House Manager Carole Wears
Deputy House Manager Michael Davies
Duty House Manager Ben Young
Duty House Manager Mark Gerrens
Duty House Manager Lewis Jobson
Duty House Manager Sarah Matthews

Front of House & Box Office Staff
Glace Blamire, Nina Berry, Danielle Burn, Camille Burridge, Lewis Gray, Claire Henderson, Caroline Liversidge, Alicia Meehan, Arthur Roberts and Anna Ryder.

Friends of Live Theatre

Iris is the third production supported by the friends of Live Theatre. Through regular financial contributions the friends play a key role in helping us to nurture and develop new writing talent and deliver plays of world-class quality.

Our Best Friends are:

Noreen Bates
Jim Beirne
Michael and Pat Brown
Dorothy Braithwaite and Paul Callaghan
George Caulkin
Michael and Susan Chaplin
Sue and Simon Clugston
Helen Coyne
Chris Foy
Stephen Garbutt
Robson Green
Lee Hall
John Jordan
John Josephs
Annette Marlowe
Madelaine Newton
Elaine Orrick
Ian and Christine Shepherdson
Margaret and John Shipley
Shelagh Stephenson
Sting
Alan Tailford
Graeme and Aly Thompson
Paul and Julie Tomlinson
Nick and Melanie Tulip
Alison Walton
Kevin Whately
Lucy Winskell

For more information about the Friends scheme please contact Lizzy Skingley on **(0191) 269 3499** or **lizzy@live.org.uk** or visit **www.live.org.uk/friends**

CAST

KATY CAVANAGH Julie

Katy trained at RADA. She recently bid a fond farewell to Weatherfield where she spent seven years playing much loved knicker-stitcher Julie Carp in *Coronation Street*. She is delighted to be making her debut at Live Theatre.

Katy's theatre credits include: *Sergeant Musgrave's Dance* (Oxford Stage Company), *Two and Two/2* (Bolton Octagon); *Ghosts, Mad For It* (Manchester Royal Exchange), *Romeo and Juliet* (English Shakespeare Company).

Her television appearances include: *Birds of a Feather* series III (BBC); *Wired* (ITV); *The Bill* (ITV); *The Street* (BBC); *Blue Murder: Crisis* (ITV); *Bodies* (BBC); *Cracker* (ITV); *The Family Man, Shameless* (C4); *The Royal, The Golden Hour, Burn It, Dalziel & Pascoe* (BBC); *Ted & Alice* (BBC), *A Line in the Sand, Bob & Rose* (ITV); *The Cops I, II & III, A Likeness in Stone* (BBC); *Holby City* (BBC); *Peak Practice* (ITV); *Sex 'n' Death* (BBC); *Where the Heart Is* (ITV); *Walter: The Secret Life, Wycliffe* (ITV); and *A Dance to the Music of Time* (Channel 4).

Her films include: *Rehab; Vacuuming Completely Nude in Paradise*; and short film *Bradford Halifax London.*

Katy has worked extensively on BBC Radio 4, most recently as Grusha in *The Brothers Karamazov* and Amelia in *Vanity Fair.*

SAM NEALE Ruby

Sam's theatre credits include: *Nativities* and *The Girls from Poppyfield Close* (Live Theatre); *Continuum* (Theatre Cap-a-Pie) and *A Bit of Respect* (Operating Theatre); *Present Tense, The Big Society* and most recently her own play with her new company Flaming Barstool Productions.

Her television credits include: *Married, Single, Other,* (Left Bank Pictures); *Vera* (ITV); *Eternal Law* (ITV); *Holby City* (BBC); *Wolfblood* (BBC) and *Doctors* (BBC).

Film credits include: *Interview with a Hitman* and *Frank.*

JOE CAFFREY Gerry

Joe trained at LAMDA. He won Performer of the Year at the 2013 Journal Culture Awards for his roles in the Live Theatre productions *Cooking with Elvis* and *Wet House.*

Theatre credits include: *The Girls* (Leeds Grand / Lowry Theatre); *Light Shining In Buckinghamshire* (National Theatre); *Cooking with Elvis* (Live Theatre); *Wet House* (Live Theatre/Soho Theatre); *The Pitmen Painters* (Live Theatre/National Theatre/Bill Kenwright Ltd, West End and National Tour); *A Walk On Part* (Live Theatre/Arts Theatre, West End), *Much Ado About Nothing, The Globe Mysteries, Loves Labours Lost* and *We the People* (Shakespeare's Globe Theatre); *Billy Elliot The Musical* (Victoria Palace Theatre); *Keepers of the Flame* (RSC/Live Theatre); *Black and White Shorts* (Live Theatre/Paines Plough); *Studs* (Hull Truck Theatre); *Cooking with Elvis* (Live Theatre West End/National Tour) and many other Live Theatre productions over the last 27 years.

Television and film credits include: *Wolfblood, Clay, Doctors, Holby City* (BBC); *The Bill* (ITV); *Heartbeat* (ITV); *Badger* (BBC); *Spender* (BBC); *Hetty Wainthrope Investigates* (BBC); *Attachments* (BBC); *Byker Grove* (BBC); *Distant Shores* (ITV); *Catherine Cookson's Colour Blind* (ITV); *Quayside* (ITV); *Waiters, The Last Musketeer* (ITV); *Ain't Misbehavin'* (BBC) and *Soldier, Soldier* (ITV); *In Fading Light* (Amber Films); *The One and Only* (Assassin Films) and *Bridget Jones – The Edge of Reason* (Working Title Films).

CREATIVE TEAM

ALISON CARR Writer

Iris is Alison's first full length commission for Live Theatre. Alison won Live Theatre's 40th Anniversary Bursary in 2013 for *The Soaking of Vera Shrimp*, which transferred to the Edinburgh Festival Fringe. Her other plays at Live Theatre include *The Girls From Poppyfield Close* and *Clint*. Her recent theatre credits include: *Fat Alice* (Traverse Theatre/Òran Mór /Aberdeen Performing Arts); *A Wondrous Place* (Northern Spirit, tour); *Never Rains But It Pours* (Theatre503) and *Can Cause Death* starring Olivier Award-winning actor David Bradley (Forward Theatre Project at the National Theatre, Northern Stage & Latitude Festival).

Alison is a member of the Traverse 50. She has also worked with theatres and companies including Paines Plough, Nabokov, Old Vic New Voices, New Writing North, Village Pub Theatre and 5065 Lift.

Radio credits include: *Dolly Would* (BBC Radio 4) and *Yackety Yak* (The Verb, BBC Radio 3).

MAX ROBERTS Artistic Director

Max is the Artistic Director and a founding member of Live Theatre.

He is delighted to be directing *Iris* by Alison Carr, who joins an esteemed list of Live Theatre authors that Max has worked with including C.P. Taylor, Tom Hadaway, Alan Plater, Phil Woods, Julia Darling, Shelagh Stephenson, Peter Straughan, Lee Hall, Michael Chaplin, Sean O'Brien, Paddy Campbell and David Almond.

Recent productions for the company include a revival of Lee Hall's *Cooking with Elvis* as part of Live Theatre's 40th anniversary celebrations; *Tyne* by Michael Chaplin which following its run at Live Theatre transferred to the Newcastle Theatre Royal; *Wet House* by Paddy Campbell which won a host of Journal Culture Awards including Best Production, and transferred to London's Soho Theatre; *Flying Into Daylight* by Ron Hutchinson; and *What Falls Apart* by Torben Betts.

Following *Iris* Max will direct *The Savage* by David Almond, an adaptation of his popular novel, which will mark the opening of Live Tales, the company's new writing centre for young people.

In 2014 Max was given an honorary doctorate of letters from Northumbria University in recognition of his work raising the International profile of theatre in the region. In 2011 Max received the Journal Culture Award's Special Contribution Award, which was given to salute his work with Live Theatre.

PATRICK CONNELLAN Designer

This is Patrick's first design for Live Theatre. Theatre credits include *Martha, Josie and The Chinese Elvis* (Hull/Bolton Octagon Theatre); *The Ladykillers* (New Vic/Hull/Stephen Joseph); *The Hook* (Royal & Derngate/Liverpool Everyman); *Three Minute Heroes, One Night in November, The Rink, A Midsummer Night's Dream* (as director and designer Edinburgh Festival), *The Dice House, This Lime Tree Bower* (as director and designer, also Edinburgh Festival); *Silas Marner, She Stoops To Conquer, Leader of the Pack, Neville's Island, The Wedding* (Coventry Belgrade); *The Taming of the Shrew, The Merchant of Venice* and *Into The Woods* (nominated for TMA Best Musical Award) (Derby Theatre/Playhouse); *20th Century Boy* (New Wolsey); *Edward III* (RSC/West End); *A Passionate Woman, Misery* (West End); *The Slight Witch* (National Theatre/Birmingham Rep); *Where Have I Been All*

My Life, Abigail's Party (as director and designer) *Copenhagen* and *Alphabetical Order* (New Vic, Stoke); *Who's Afraid of Virginia Woolf, The Price, Ghosts, All My Sons, The Seafarer, Meet the Mukherjees, Popcorn* (as director and designer) (MEN Award), *Broken Glass, Twelfth Night, Little Malcolm, The Weir* and *The Hypochondriac* (Bolton Octagon Theatre) and for Hampstead Theatre: *Amongst Friends, Life After Scandal* (also Plymouth), *Taking Care of Baby* (also Birmingham Rep), *The Maths Tutor, Osama the Hero/A Single Act, My Best Friend* (also Birmingham Rep), *Nathan the Wise* and *When the Night Begins.*

Patrick is currently designing *The Baraem Play* for Al Jazeera Media Networks; *Roll over Beethoven* for Belgrade Theatre, Coventry; and *The Gaul* for Hull Truck.

Patrick has previously won the Linbury Prize for Stage Design and a Prague Quadriennale Gold Medal. Until recently, Patrick was the Course Leader of Theatre Design at Nottingham Trent University and now teaches theatre design at Royal Welsh College of Music and Drama.

LUCY JENKINS CDG & SOOKI MCSHANE CDG Casting Directors

Live Theatre credits include: *Tyne, Cooking with Elvis, Chalet Lines, A Walk On Part, Nativities, Faith & Cold Reading, Inheritance* and *A Northern Odyssey.*

Other theatre credits include: *To Kill a Mockingbird* (Regents Park and tour), *The Man Who Shot Liberty Valance, Desdemona, Bomber's Moon, Adult Supervision* and *Casualties* (Park Theatre); *Our Country's Good* (Out Of Joint); *Much Ado About Nothing* (Royal Exchange Theatre); *Moon on a Rainbow Shawl* (Talawa Theatre); *War Horse* (UK Tour/West End), *Solid Air* (Theatre Royal Plymouth); *Afraid of the Dark* (Charing Cross Theatre); *Serpent's Tooth* (Almeida Theatre/Talawa Theatre); *The Glee Club* (Cast Theatre) and several productions for Nottingham Playhouse including *The Kite Runner, My Judy Garland Life, Richard III, The Ashes* and *Diary of a Football Nobody.*

Television credits include: *Skins* (Company Pictures); *Wild At Heart* (Company Pictures); *The Bill* (Talkback Thames); *Samuel Johnson: The Dictionary Man* (October Films) and *Family Affairs* (Talkback Thames).

Film credits include: *Myrrdin* (Screenworks); *Awaiting* (Solar Productions); *Containment* (Bright Cold Day Films); *Five-A-Side* (Emerald Films); *Entity* (Nexus DNA); *The Somnambulists* (No Bad Films); *Desi Boyz* (Desi Boyz Productions) and H10 (Dan Films).

A word from the writer

Iris started its life as a twenty-minute short called, believe it or not, '*Iris*'. In it, warring sisters Julie and Ruby met in a café to meet with a woman who was delivering the bequest of their recently deceased mother Iris.

I can't tell you what that bequest is (spoilers) but suffice to say it's a bit, well, odd. But then my plays often contain the unusual. A boy who believes he has an 'inside twin' growing inside him who only he can hear; a grossly obese upstairs neighbour's massive foot crashing into an adulterous couple's living room; a mother who replaces her child with a stuffed monkey toy. Of course, these stories are rarely actually about the weird thing that's happening, and I enjoy putting the extreme into the ordinary to see where it leads me and my characters.

This short play sat in a drawer for a few years until I was looking to write a full length script. The central conceit was interesting, but there was a lot more in there to explore and discover. The sisters had a significant age gap between them, how did this affect their relationship? Why was this family estranged? Who was this mother and why had she done this? On and on it went until Julie was a Cher impersonator amongst a cast of six in a four act play called *The Day We Rode The Shuggy Boat*. Ahead of Live Theatre's final *Short Cuts* event back in 2012 during which they showcased a scene from this epic, I spent a day workshopping the script with actors and a director. A lot became clear. Not only has the title reverted back to its original since then (it had to, Iris is such a force even if she's unseen) but it's a lot trimmer, half the characters have been culled and there's not a Cher classic to be heard.

In the redrafting, the play became less and less about the weirdness of Iris's bequest and increasingly about the family in which this would be a thing that could happen. It opened up to ideas about sisterhood, motherhood, legacy, loss, blame, and all that big, juicy stuff.

Older sister Julie came to the fore, her relationship with Iris and Ruby, her sense of self, her guilt. Julie is one of those oft discussed lately 'strong female leads'. Not 'strong' as in infallible cos that's not interesting or human, but 'strong' as in central, the heart of this story. She's in her mid-forties, an intelligent, funny, conflicted, damaged woman whose decisions and mistakes have got her to this point and now it's all imploding. She, along with Ruby and Gerry, are not always right or likable, but that's ok. They're people who are coping (or failing to) with – in the words of Ruby – "a pretty fucking creepy" situation.

How the play was going to end prompted a lot of discussion. As it is, nothing is tied up in a nice neat bow, all rainbows and lollipops, but what is? There's hope. And that's something.

Alison Carr
Writer

Iris

by

Alison Carr

ISBN 978-0-573-11234-8

www.samuelfrench-london.co.uk
www.samuelfrench.com

Back cover copy written by Literary Manager Gez Casey

FOR AMATEUR PRODUCTION ENQUIRIES

UNITED KINGDOM AND WORLD EXCLUDING NORTH AMERICA

plays@SamuelFrench-London.co.uk

020 7255 4302/01

Each title is subject to availability from Samuel French, depending upon country of performance.

Please note that text was correct at time of rehearsal and may differ from the live performance.

CHARACTERS

Julie
The elder of the two sisters. 45.
She can seem cold and distant. She doesn't like mess.

Ruby
The younger of the two. 19. She can be brattish and crude.

Gerry
In his mid-40s, a recently divorced dad-of-one
who is looking for love.

SETTING

The living room of a house.

A settee.

A low coffee table – it bears the leftovers of platters of food for a buffet.

Chairs around a small dining table with more leftovers, paper plates, paper cups and a cluster of half drunk or empty wine and spirit bottles.

In a corner on the floor is a pile of post – junk mail mostly, that is piled on top of a large square parcel still sealed tightly in its packaging.

One wall is covered with mirrors of various shapes, sizes and ages. There is a noticeable gap where a mirror once hung – there is an outline, the wallpaper less faded where it once was.

There are two doors. One, the front door off to outside.
The other to the kitchen.

There is a window with a view on to the street.

A staircase leads off upstairs to the bedrooms and bathroom.

ACT ONE

Scene One

The very early hours of the morning.

The room is in darkness.

JULIE *and* **GERRY** *are heard outside.* **JULIE** *is fumbling with her door keys –.*

GERRY *(offstage)* Shall I shine my phone?

JULIE *(offstage)* It's ok.

GERRY *(offstage)* Here, look…

JULIE *(offstage)* I've got it…

JULIE *opens the front door. They enter.*

JULIE *wears a smart black dress and heels.* **GERRY** *is smart too, but not a suit. They have both had a drink.*

I had the key upside down.

GERRY Silly.

JULIE Yeah.

GERRY Dafty, aren't you. Dafty.

A right silly sausage.

This breaks the mood. **JULIE** *moves away.*

JULIE I need a top up.

Get some lights on, eh.

JULIE *turns the light on and examines the leftover bottles on the table –.*

There's some vodka. Oh no, that's empty.

This? No idea what it is, but if you're feeling brave…

GERRY Just a glass of water, if I can.

JULIE Just water? Cos I'm having this…

GERRY Best not.

JULIE You haven't had that much.

GERRY We've had quite a bit.

JULIE No.

I thought you said you were off work tomorrow…?

GERRY I am.

JULIE Right then.

GERRY Really, not for me.

JULIE Spoilsport.

Exit **JULIE** *to the kitchen.*

GERRY *mooches. He takes his coat off – drapes it over a chair.*

He is drawn to the wall covered in mirrors.

Enter **JULIE** *with a glass of water.*

She catches **GERRY** *preening himself –.*

GERRY Busted.

JULIE Here.

GERRY This is different. Very unique.

I like it.

JULIE *doesn't look at the mirrors. She moves away, sits down.*

GERRY *doesn't notice, remains.*

Apparently women spend fifty-five minutes a day looking at themselves.

That's two weeks a year. Think of what more you could –

Oh, you've gone.

JULIE Can you smell something a bit off?

GERRY No.

JULIE Are you sure?

GERRY Yeah.

JULIE …

He joins her on the settee.

GERRY Cheers. Clink.

JULIE …

GERRY *(re the water)* Delicious.

JULIE It's just out the tap.

GERRY Right.

JULIE Do you want some more?

GERRY I'm fine, thanks.

Pause.

I took my coat off.

JULIE Ok.

GERRY I wasn't sure where to put it…

JULIE There's fine.

GERRY Have you been throwing a party? *(The platters)*

JULIE No.

GERRY You're not a silly sausage.

JULIE What?

GERRY Before. I don't know why I said it…

JULIE It's alright.

GERRY It happens. If I'm nervous. Blathering on…

JULIE It's fine.

GERRY …on and on and on, like a right pillock.

JULIE Yeah.

GERRY Yeah.

They kiss.

GERRY*'s hand edges under her dress – she moves it away. He tries again and she breaks away –.*

You alright?

JULIE Yeah. Fine. Great.

Kissing resumes.

He continues to try to undress her. She pulls away again –

GERRY What's wrong?

JULIE Nothing.

Nothing.

JULIE *jumps up and grabs a platter off the coffee table –.*

Clear this up. Not nice for you, stale vol-au-vents wherever you look…

JULIE *heads for the kitchen.*

GERRY stands and retrieves his coat.

What are you doing?

GERRY Going home.

JULIE Why?

GERRY I thought you asked me back to… I've obviously misunderstood.

He goes to the door.

JULIE Wait. Just… Let me nip upstairs.

GERRY No, I'm sorry.

He hesitates at the doorway –.

When you rang… Out of the blue, like that. I never thought you would ring. I was just plating up a pasta bake. I left it. Dropped everything. Because I thought… I really hoped. I'm sorry.

JULIE I can't be on my own, not tonight.

Please.

JULIE pulls a couple of "chicken fillets" from her bra / she hoiks up her dress and pulls off a pair of ugly support pants.

Maybe Bridget Jones can make them sexy, but not me.

GERRY Is that it?

JULIE It's embarrassing. Imagine if you had a sock in your boxers, I stuck my hand in and pulled it out.

GERRY I'd just be glad you had your hand in my boxers.

JULIE This is a clingy fabric. And the cut, it needs shape and I…

I wanted to look nice.

GERRY You look beautiful.

JULIE She never liked what I wear.

I think this would get approval, though. I thought today, for her, try and do something she wouldn't find fault with.

GERRY Let's start again.

JULIE What?

GERRY Clean slate. Come on.

GERRY *grabs her and pulls her outside –.*

JULIE Yes, but – Hang on, my –

He slams the front door closed behind them.

(Outside) My keys.

GERRY *(outside)* What?

JULIE *(outside)* My door keys. They're on the table.

GERRY *(outside)* Oh. Is there a window open? I could shimmy up the drainpipe.

JULIE *(outside)* No.

JULIE *starts ringing on the doorbell.*

GERRY *(outside)* Who's in?

JULIE *(outside)* Ruby.

GERRY *(outside)* Who's Ruby?

JULIE *leans on the bell – it rings unrelentingly.*

(Outside) Is she definitely in?

JULIE *(outside)* Yes.

GERRY *(outside)* Some people can sleep through all sorts. A gas works went up near my uncle, he slept right through.

JULIE *(outside)* She can hear me.

Enter **RUBY** *from upstairs.*

She wears a dressing gown over pyjamas. She wears an eye-patch (which she wears throughout the play).

RUBY Who is it?

JULIE *pokes the letterbox open – talks through it.*

JULIE *(outside)* It's me. Open this door.

RUBY *opens the door.*

Enter **JULIE** *and* **GERRY**.

GERRY Thank you. Ruby, is it? Sorry to get you up, my fault…

RUBY *exits upstairs, ignoring him.*

Nothing worse when you're happily snoozing in the land of nod.

Sorry.

GERRY *and* **JULIE** *remain, awkward – him in his coat, her holding her support pants.*

JULIE If you want to go. Try and salvage that pasta bake.

GERRY Do you want me to go?

JULIE It's up to you.

GERRY You say.

JULIE I'd like you to stay.

GERRY Really?

JULIE I just said, didn't I?

GERRY You're sure?

JULIE Yes.

Yes.

GERRY Ok then.

JULIE Ok. Good.

GERRY Good.

JULIE Good.

Scene Two

The same day – late morning.

RUBY *is sitting on the sofa in her dressing gown eating her breakfast. The telly is on – something loud and obnoxious.*

The food/drink leftovers from the day before remain.

Enter **JULIE** *from upstairs.*

JULIE Morning.

RUBY …

JULIE *finds the remote – reduces the volume.*

I'm watching that.

JULIE It's blasting.

Exit **JULIE** *to the kitchen. She calls through to* **RUBY** *(who has turned the telly volume back up) –.*

What do you do in here? How is it possible to make toasting a slice of bread a cataclysmic event?

Ruby.

Ruby.

RUBY I can hear you.

JULIE Good. And stop putting empty milk cartons back in the fucking fridge.

JULIE *returns with a glass of water.*

She turns the telly back down.

Oi.

RUBY Yes.

JULIE *(re the platters/bottles)* You could have made a start chucking these.

RUBY The bin's full.

JULIE Put them out then.

RUBY Green bin's full too.

JULIE That smell is definitely getting worse…rotteny. Comes and goes.

RUBY It'll be this lot. *(She sniffs at the platters)*

JULIE *(pointedly)* I'll get some bin bags then, shall I? Make a start?

RUBY You bought it all, not me.

Exit **JULIE** *to the kitchen.*

(Mimicking **JULIE***)* "We have to put a spread on. There's always a spread, people will want feeding".

RUBY *ups the telly volume louder still.*

Enter **JULIE** *with bin bags. She sets about clearing up.*

JULIE *(re the bottles of booze)* We'll keep all the spirits and anything unopened.

RUBY Sorry what? I can't hear you, the telly's quite loud.

JULIE *wrestles the remote from her and turns the telly off.*

RUBY *watches* **JULIE** *tidy –.*

Good night?

JULIE There was me panicking we wouldn't have enough food.

RUBY It took me ages to realise you'd gone.

JULIE What a waste.

RUBY What time did you leave?

Julie.

JULIE I'm not sure. It was down to the last few.

RUBY I didn't top up any glasses or walk round with trays of nibbles.

JULIE I never imagined you would.

RUBY They were all staring at me, whispering.

JULIE No they weren't.

(Re the bottles) Can you go and pour these out please,

RUBY I went up to my room and stayed there.

JULIE Best thing.

RUBY So where is the poor sod?

Did he peel himself off your stinking sheets and leg it first thing?

Or maybe you've killed him and eaten him like one of them spiders?

Exit **JULIE** *to the kitchen.*

RUBY *pulls* **JULIE***'s black dress from the night before out from under a settee cushion.*

She's not even cold, Julie.

Enter **JULIE**. *She clocks the dress –.*

She's not even cold.

JULIE Give it here.

RUBY You looked so prim and proper in it at the service, who would believe it.

He's ruined it. It's definitely going to stain.

JULIE *snatches the dress off her and exits upstairs.*

(Shouting after her) You're upset over a few crumbs in the kitchen, but you'll happily let him shoot his load all over you.

We hear a fumble of keys in the front door from outside. The front door opens.

Julie! Julie!

Panicked, **RUBY** *bolts to the door – slams it closed.*

GERRY *(outside)* Oouf.

RUBY Who is it?

GERRY *(outside)* It's me.

RUBY Oh well, in that case…

GERRY *(outside)* Gerry.

From last night.

RUBY *tentatively opens the door.*

GERRY*'s wearing the same clothes from the night before. He's clutching his nose and carrying a plastic bag containing provisions.*

Hiya.

He enters and moves across to the mirrors – examines his face for damage.

RUBY One shag and she's giving you keys to the place.

GERRY I took them off the table.

RUBY How very presumptuous of you.

GERRY No-one was up, I didn't want to leave the place standing open.

I'm sorry if I gave you a fright.

RUBY You didn't.

GERRY *(re his nose/face)* I think it's ok. No uglier than before, eh.

RUBY …

GERRY *(re mirrors)* I hope your missing one didn't get broken.

RUBY It did, actually.

GERRY Oh dear. Seven years bad luck.

Unless you bury the pieces, apparently. Under a tree during a full moon.

Or grind them to dust. Apparently.

RUBY Julie swept them up and put them in the bin.

GERRY Wrapped in newspaper I hope.

RUBY …

GERRY I was just saying to your…erm…to Julie last night, I like it –

RUBY Yeah?

GERRY That seventies looking one – I think we had that in our house growing up.

RUBY That one's charity shop. That one's quite recent, IKEA. That one Mam found in a skip when someone down the street was getting their garage done.

GERRY Why mirrors?

RUBY Why not? Some people collect stamps, Mam likes mirrors. She says "we should always be able to look ourselves in the eye".

GERRY Good advice.

Silence. Eventually –.

It's just the two of you living here, then, is it?

RUBY Yes.

GERRY No brothers or sisters?

Enter **JULIE** *from upstairs. She is not expecting to see* **GERRY** *back.*

JULIE Oh. Hello.

GERRY Morning.

RUBY He's back.

JULIE So I see.

GERRY Like a bad penny.

It's ok, isn't it?

RUBY Course.

GERRY I don't come empty handed.

Milk, I saw you were running low. Bread, eggs –

JULIE You didn't have to.

GERRY Happy to.

Beans –

RUBY Uh-oh.

GERRY No?

RUBY She finds them sinister.

JULIE It's something about the texture.

GERRY Noted.

RUBY This is so generous. Isn't it Julie, so generous.

JULIE Yes, thank you…erm… I'm sure I can rustle us something up. Do you want a cuppa?

RUBY Yes please.

JULIE Not you.

(To **GERRY***)* Tea or coffee?

RUBY Tea please.

JULIE I'm not asking you, I'm asking… *(But she can't remember his name)*

GERRY Gerry.

JULIE Gerry.

I'll put this away, shall I. *(The shopping)*

Was it tea or coffee?

GERRY Tea.

Exit **JULIE** *to the kitchen.*

RUBY Please. Take the weight off.

They sit.

Did you manage to avoid the dog shit on the doorstep?

GERRY I hope so.

RUBY It's a bastard terrier from the top of the street. We think it's been trained to empty its bowels outside our house.

GERRY *(checks his shoes)* All clear.

Enter **JULIE**. *She tidies some more.*

JULIE Kettle's just boiling.

RUBY I was just telling Gerry about the dog. Angelic little face, toxic arse.

JULIE Nice.

RUBY If you will leave me making small talk with your sexual conquests.

GERRY *(re* **JULIE** *tidying)* Can I help you with that?

JULIE It's fine.

GERRY I thought we could go for a walk later.

You too of course, Ruby, if you'd like.

RUBY No thanks.

GERRY It's a lovely day.

RUBY And?

GERRY Ok. Well, maybe us two. The beach maybe? It must be nice having it so close.

JULIE No.

GERRY No the beach or no the walk?

JULIE Let's just see how we feel later on.

RUBY She'll let you thrash her gash all night, but going for a walk with you…that needs some serious thought.

JULIE Sorry.

GERRY Your… *(He gestures to her patch/cheek)*

RUBY What?

GERRY You've got something…it's seeping.

RUBY *goes to the mirrors.*

JULIE Is it hurting?

RUBY No.

JULIE Don't wipe it on your sleeve. That's why it gets infected.

Have you been putting the lotion on?

RUBY Yes.

Get it for me, then. It's in the bathroom.

Exit **JULIE** *upstairs.*

GERRY It is a stye? My brother gets styes.

RUBY …

GERRY Warm water compress, stops it crusting over.

RUBY Yeah?

GERRY With a vinegar soak. We swear by them in our family.

RUBY If you've got experience, Gerry…could you look at it for me?

GERRY Of course.

RUBY It started off going really red, and then –

She lifts the patch up right in his face, just a flash.

JULIE *returns with cotton wool pads/lotion in time to see this.*

Gone!

GERRY Jesus Christ.

JULIE For fuck's sake, Ruby.

RUBY A vinegar soak'll make it grow back, yeah?

JULIE Apologise.

RUBY No.

GERRY No, please. It was my fault. I got a fright. Sorry.

JULIE What are you playing at?

RUBY He thinks you're my mother.

JULIE What?

RUBY You do, don't you.

GERRY I just… I wasn't sure if…

RUBY We're sisters.

GERRY Right.

RUBY She's staggeringly older than me.

GERRY It's fine. I mean… I wouldn't have minded. How can I? I'm a dad myself.

RUBY Aw, really?

GERRY Matty. He's seven.

RUBY You alright, Julie?

JULIE Fine.

RUBY *(to* **JULIE***)* You look a bit sick.

GERRY He's a great lad.

RUBY Is he?

GERRY Do you want to see a photo?

RUBY Yes.

JULIE No.

GERRY His mum and I… I mean, we're not… I'm not running around behind her back here or anything.

RUBY I'd hope not.

GERRY We had a good run. Ten years, you think you're home and dry but…

Paula's great, a great mum. She's got twins on the way with her new fella.

But Matty, he's a special boy, he needs more looking after, more love. We meet his parenting needs better if we're apart.

RUBY You talk like a self-help manual, Gerry.

GERRY Do I?

RUBY It's either brilliant or horrific. I'm yet to decide.

GERRY Ok.

RUBY Julie's husband's called Matthew. He's a big bruiser, you might want to start running now.

JULIE Ex-husband. Very ex. Thank God.

RUBY Isn't it tacky when exes don't get on.

GERRY Everyone's relationship is different. Unless there's children involved, and then, well…

Did you and Matthew –?

JULIE No.

That kettle will be boiled. How do you have it?

GERRY Milk, half a sugar.

Exit **JULIE** *to the kitchen.*

RUBY How's your Paula going to feel about this one, eh? Although, twins, it doesn't sound like she's pining after you.

GERRY We wish each other every happiness.

Enter **JULIE.**

JULIE *(to* **GERRY***)* Do you want a biscuit?

GERRY Lovely.

Exit **JULIE** *to the kitchen.*

RUBY I knew you were called Gerry.

GERRY Sorry?

Enter **JULIE** *with tea things and biscuits.*

She invites **GERRY** *to sit with her at the dining table.* **RUBY** *remains on the settee.*

RUBY Before. When Suzy Slut here couldn't even remember your name, I knew.

JULIE Enough.

Ignore her. I'm not good with names.

RUBY Cocks, though. She's good with cocks.

JULIE Shut up.

Sugar?

RUBY I knew from what she was heavy-breathing through the wall last night that it was either "Gerry" or "Big Boy".

JULIE I never called you "Big Boy".

RUBY That's you told, eh Jezza.

Honestly, though, I'm mortified. Coming staggering home with some random she meets in a bar. No offence.

I had no idea this is how she goes on.

JULIE Biscuit?

RUBY I don't see her very much, you see.

GERRY Delicious.

RUBY She lives down the country, did she tell you that?

GERRY No.

RUBY Did the accent not give it away? Dumped it like she dumped us.

She's not stopping. Been here the best part of a month, still barely unpacked her suitcase.

GERRY How long are you staying for?

JULIE I'm not sure at the moment.

RUBY She never visits. But here she is, dragged back to the house she grew up in.

And now, screwing strange men in her childhood bedroom. Did the Holly Hobbie wallpaper not put you off your stroke? Or maybe you enjoyed it.

JULIE Right, that's it. Get upstairs, now.

RUBY Aw, I'm just messing on. You're ok Gerry, aren't you. You know I'm joking.

GERRY Yes.

RUBY See.

GERRY We didn't meet in a bar, though.

RUBY No? It wasn't a club, was it? I can't imagine you dancing.

GERRY I'm a good dancer. I've done evening classes.

RUBY I'm sure you have.

GERRY It was the other morning, wasn't it. I was standing behind her at the cash point and her bag strap broke – everything fell out. I helped her pick it up.

I gave her my number and…

JULIE You didn't give me your number.

GERRY Well, I mean, sort of.

JULIE Not really.

GERRY Is this our first row?

JULIE I got home and it was on a scrap of paper in my pocket. I'm still not sure how you did it.

GERRY A magician never gives away his secrets.

RUBY So, erm, sorry, you rang him and chose last night for a first date?

GERRY She doesn't give much notice, does your sister.

JULIE It wasn't like that. I went outside for some air. I put my hand in my pocket – the piece of paper was still there. I didn't plan to… It was a difficult day.

RUBY Wasn't it.

JULIE I'd had it all to do myself, didn't I. I just… I needed to be away.

RUBY Cos you know what else happened yesterday, Gerry.

GERRY No.

RUBY Our mam who loves the mirrors…

GERRY Yes.

RUBY We buried her.

GERRY Oh.

RUBY It was a lovely service. I imagine it was, I didn't go, but she'd laid all the arrangements out in her will so I'm sure it was perfect.

Some of the dirt Julie threw on the coffin might still have been under her nails as she scratched them down your back last night. We had the wake here. Friends and family quietly paying their last respects, but she had better places to be, left us all –

JULIE "All", they were hardly out lining the streets.

RUBY We kept to ourselves. We didn't need anyone else.

GERRY …

RUBY You had no idea, did you?

GERRY No.

RUBY Not a fucking word.

JULIE *(to* **GERRY***)* There's some bacon in, I could do you an egg and bacon sandwich?

GERRY I'm vegetarian.

RUBY Your beefy flaps, Julie, put him off meat for life.

JULIE *(to* **GERRY***)* Come through.

Exit **JULIE** *and* **GERRY** *to the kitchen.*

RUBY *remains.*

Scene Three

A few days later. Late afternoon.

RUBY *lies asleep on the sofa.*

The telly is on, loud.

The curtains are drawn. There are dirty plates and cups on the table. Post and junk mail lies on the mat.

We hear keys in the front door.

Enter **JULIE**. *She has her coat on, carries a plastic supermarket carrier bag.*

She turns the telly off.

She watches **RUBY** *sleeping. Eventually she approaches her tentatively, strokes her hair lightly.*

RUBY *starts to stir.*

RUBY Mam?

Mam?

JULIE *darts away – busies herself.*

JULIE It's alright for some, napping in the afternoons.

RUBY You.

JULIE *(opening the curtains/window)* Jesus, it's ripe in here.

RUBY Can you shut that please, it's cold.

JULIE Get some air circulating.

RUBY What do you care, you'll be going out again in a minute.

RUBY *curls back up to sleep –* **JULIE** *shakes her.*

JULIE No. Come on wake up.

RUBY Get off.

JULIE Get up, come on.

RUBY Fuck off, don't touch me.

RUBY *sits up, groggy.*

Where have you been?

JULIE Out.

RUBY Where? Last I knew, you went out for a walk with Geraldo.

JULIE I've been back to check on you.

RUBY To change your manky knickers.

JULIE It's not my fault if you sleep all day.

RUBY You haven't slept one night this week in your own bed.

JULIE It hasn't been a week. A couple of days.

RUBY Three days.

JULIE I'm here now, aren't I.

RUBY Get me a glass of water, will you. My mouth's really dry.

JULIE Are you alright?

RUBY I'm fine.

JULIE Then you know where the tap is, don't you.

RUBY *checks the cups on the tables for dregs – drinks them down.* **JULIE** *watches her, unimpressed.*

You could have at least picked up the post. *(She sorts through it)*

Junk. Junk. A couple for Iris.

RUBY Add them to the pile. *(The post pile on top of the box)*

JULIE We need to go through all that.

We need to go through all her stuff, what to keep, what to charity shop –

RUBY There's no rush.

JULIE We should get on it.

RUBY But not yet.

JULIE *(re a "missed delivery" card)* When did this come?

RUBY Yesterday.

JULIE Where were you?

RUBY Here.

JULIE Why didn't you answer the door if you were in?

RUBY I didn't know who it was.

JULIE Open the door and find out. That's how doors work.

I'll have to go to the depot now.

(Reading the delivery card) Hang on.

Exit **JULIE** *to the kitchen. She returns with a squishy package.*

He threw it over the hedge into the back garden.

RUBY What is it?

JULIE Nothing.

RUBY Let's see.

JULIE *opens it and pulls out a brightly patterned cardigan.*

Bloody hell, that's woke me up.

JULIE Don't you like it?

RUBY Put it on.

Don't face me straight on, it's blinding me in my good eye.

JULIE I thought it'd make a change, a bit colour.

RUBY You've certainly ticked that box.

JULIE I'll send it back tomorrow.

RUBY No. It's nice.

JULIE Yeah?

RUBY Yeah. Now I'm acclimatising.

I mean, it looks like a rainbow's thrown up all over you. But it suits you.

JULIE Do you think I should ring Joseph?

RUBY Who's Joseph?

JULIE Own up to nicking his Amazing Technicolour Dreamcoat.

RUBY Ha! *(Singing from Joseph and his Amazing Technicolour Dreamcoat)*

JULIE *(joining in)*

It's a bit rich, mind.

RUBY What is?

JULIE You critiquing what I wear. That dressing gown's going to crawl off your back soon, drag itself to the washing machine.

RUBY It's fine.

JULIE It's you reeking the place out, stinker.

RUBY Shut up.

Silence. Any hint of friendship/getting along has gone.

JULIE You've never had a sense of smell.

RUBY There's nothing to smell.

JULIE There is. It's stronger when you come in from outside.

RUBY Why don't you sort it out then, instead of bleating on about it.

RUBY *goes to turn the telly back on.*

JULIE No. Tidy your mess up, please. I'm not having you festering in your pit when Gerry's here.

RUBY He's coming round?

JULIE Yes.

RUBY You've spent the last week with him.

JULIE Not a week.

RUBY Can't you stay in tonight?

JULIE I am.

RUBY Just you.

JULIE But then where would you go?

RUBY When's he coming over?

JULIE About eight.

RUBY What am I meant to do? Sit here while you two neck on?

JULIE It's up to you.

RUBY Are you cooking?

JULIE I got one of those meal deals for a tenner.

RUBY What did you get?

JULIE *passes her the bag.*

JULIE All that for a tenner. And wine. It's probably like paint stripper but still. Tenner.

RUBY I don't like broccoli.

JULIE It's not for you.

RUBY What am I meant to have? I'm starving.

JULIE There's cupboards full. You watched me carry it all in last week.

RUBY I haven't had any fruit or veg in ages. I've probably got scurvy.

JULIE There's fruit and veg in.

RUBY Rotten.

JULIE I'll make you something. What do you want?

RUBY So I have to choke down your muck, but he's spared.

JULIE Sort yourself out, then. The shop's just over the road.

RUBY Tell me something about him.

JULIE Like what?

RUBY Anything.

Does he live in a grimy bedsit? Or a half-way house. Are guests frowned upon while they regenerate him back into the community?

JULIE Reintegrate.

RUBY So it is that, then?

JULIE No. Look, I'll go to his if you want. But you're the one moaning that I'm never here.

RUBY Why are you even bothering? He lives up here, you're down there. There's no future. Unless. If you're staying?

JULIE It's just a bit of fun, isn't it.

RUBY Does he know that? I've seen how he looks at you.

JULIE And how's that?

RUBY Like a really ugly pigeon eyeing up a mangy old chip. What's his job?

JULIE What does it matter?

RUBY If he's in your life, he's in mine. That's how it is now.

JULIE He's a cleaner.

What's that face for?

RUBY Nothing. Now you say it, he does look like a man who's seen some toilets. Haunted eyes.

JULIE Not toilets. Crime scenes. It's very specialist.

RUBY Like CSI?

JULIE No. The aftermath.

RUBY Blood?

JULIE Amongst other things.

RUBY What kind of freak has a job like that?

JULIE Some people like to work for a living. Not lie around in their dressing gowns all day.

RUBY Give it a rest.

JULIE Oh you can dish it out –

RUBY Fine, I'll tidy up like a good little slave for you and your weirdo boyfriend.

JULIE He's not my boyfriend.

RUBY *carries a mug to the kitchen.*

(Calling after her) Don't strain yourself.

JULIE *makes to clear the rest.*

She notices a dark stain on a settee cushion.

What's this?

Have you spilt something?

(Sniffs at it) Have you…?

Fuck's sake, Ruby. Ruby.

Enter **RUBY**.

RUBY What?

JULIE *spins her round – she yanks off the dressing gown. The back of* **RUBY**'*s joggers are wet.*

JULIE Look at this.

RUBY What?

I didn't realise.

JULIE How can you not realise you've pissed your pants? Sitting there in it –

JULIE *pulls the cushions out. She finds a bottle of tablets.*

What's this?

Are these yours?

RUBY Yes.

JULIE They're Iris's.

RUBY They're just sleeping tablets.

JULIE Prescribed. Her dose, prescribed for her.

How many have you had?

RUBY One.

Three at most.

JULIE No wonder you were conked out. Are you stupid?

RUBY I just wanted to get some sleep.

JULIE Close your eyes and count sheep.

RUBY Oh yeah, I bet you're out like a light.

JULIE Yes, I sleep alright actually. Cos I go out, I see people, I do things. But you. You must have some friends you knock about with?

RUBY There's no-one round here worth being friends with.

JULIE On the computer, then?

RUBY You want me to get groomed?

JULIE At least you'd be talking to somebody.

You don't need pills, you need to get off your arse. Do something. Anything.

RUBY This house is too big with just me. Too still.

I've never spent a night here on my own before. It creaks. The pipes whine. And every night you haven't come back it's gotten louder.

I had to block it out, shut my brain off.

JULIE This is dangerous.

RUBY Stay home and I'll stop.

JULIE This ends now.

Get in the shower, get changed. I'll cancel Gerry.

RUBY Why?

JULIE We're going out. Fresh air, a change of scenery.

RUBY I can't.

JULIE You can.

RUBY I'm not ready.

JULIE For what? It's just outside.

JULIE *throws the door open.*

See. Just air and sky and pavement.

RUBY I haven't been outside since she died.

JULIE That's what I'm saying.

You've needed time, ok, but enough's enough.

(Stepping outside) Look, it's fine. No bolts of lightning, I'm still in one piece.

Just stand on the path if you like, get some colour in your cheeks.

Ruby. Now.

Iris might have let you get away with being a little madam, but not me. Come on.

JULIE *tries to grab at her but* **RUBY** *slams the door closed.*

(Outside) Ruby!

RUBY If she knew she was going to die she should have told me.

JULIE *(outside)* What? She didn't know.

RUBY Then why was everything arranged? What flowers, what music, the coffin.

JULIE *(outside)* You know how she was, her way or no way.

RUBY Why did we have to wait so long for her body?

JULIE *(outside)* When a person dies at home… I don't know.

JULIE*'s phone beeps.*

RUBY Your phone's beeping.

It's Gerry.

JULIE *(outside)* Don't read it.

RUBY Please. I don't want to see his dick pic. I've got enough going on.

JULIE *(outside)* Open the door.

RUBY Do you miss her?

JULIE *(outside)* Yes.

RUBY You don't seem like you do.

JULIE *(outside)* Ruby

RUBY Be honest and I'll let you back in.

JULIE *(outside)* I don't think it's sunk in that she's dead. It's not like I saw her that often, it still just feels like that, like she's about to walk into the room.

RUBY When was the last time you saw her?

JULIE *(outside)* I came up… I can't remember.

RUBY I can. Ages ago.

We had lamb. You had a strop cos you dripped mint sauce on your new jumper. She always made a lovely Sunday dinner.

JULIE *(outside)* She did, yeah.

RUBY I miss her. Not like you. I know she's gone, absolutely and totally gone, and that's worse. When it hits you… You'll see.

Some days I feel so heavy with it, like my arms and legs are concrete. Others, everything churns around inside me, too fast, making my head spin. Is that normal? Julie?

Julie?

Enter **JULIE** *from the kitchen.*

JULIE Backdoor key under the plant pot. Learnt my lesson after last time.

RUBY I'm talking to you. I'm trying to tell you how I feel.

JULIE *retrieves her phone.*

JULIE Gerry wants to know if he can come by a bit earlier.

There's nothing stopping him is there?

RUBY I thought you were cancelling?

JULIE No need if you won't come out.

I'll tell him about an hour. Give you a chance to clean yourself up.

RUBY …

JULIE I know you miss Iris. It's a process. You'll feel what you feel when you feel it. And if you're not prepared to help yourself…

RUBY Great advice. Maybe get it printed on a tea towel.

JULIE Maybe I will.

RUBY Mam was right about you.

JULIE Dare I ask?

RUBY Selfish.

JULIE Of course.

RUBY I mean, how am I supposed to know? I don't know you, you're practically a stranger.

JULIE All I've done since I got here is run around after you.

RUBY All you've done is whinge and slag yourself out to the first imbecile who'll have you while I sit here starving, full of pills and covered in piss.

JULIE …

RUBY Mam wouldn't want him here, so…

JULIE Well she's not here, so…

RUBY I hate you.

JULIE Let's not, ok.

RUBY I fucking loathe you.

JULIE I thought I was a stranger?

RUBY You are.

JULIE If you're not using the shower, then I am.

RUBY I wish you'd died.

JULIE Don't say that.

RUBY Already done. What you going to do about it?

JULIE I've tried to be nice.

RUBY This is you trying to be nice?

JULIE You make it very difficult.

RUBY My mam is dead, can't you say something kind to me?

JULIE …

RUBY I have nothing, no-one. You said so yourself.

JULIE You've got everything. It's all ahead of you. Start making plans.

RUBY About what?

JULIE How you're going to support yourself, where you're going to live.

RUBY Here.

JULIE Maybe. You'd live here on your own?

RUBY No.

JULIE Sell it, then? Move somewhere new.

RUBY No.

JULIE See.

Nothing has to be set in stone right now. But we – you – have to start thinking about it at least.

RUBY And what if I don't?

JULIE That's not an option.

RUBY Yes it is. If do nothing, then it's an option.

JULIE I can't stay up here indefinitely. I've got a job, a flat, things to do that I've just left hanging.

RUBY You can live here.

JULIE No.

RUBY You can work here – people need to learn to drive up here too. We have roads, traffic lights, corners that need reversing around.

JULIE It's not as simple as that.

RUBY Why not?

JULIE Because it's not.

RUBY That's not an answer.

JULIE Because I don't want to.

My life isn't this. It isn't here and it isn't you.

RUBY You'll leave me.

JULIE I didn't say that.

RUBY You just did.

JULIE *doesn't reply.* **RUBY** *gets right in her face.*

Fuck, you will as well.

(Staring in her eyes) There's nothing there, just black. Not a flicker.

JULIE *tries to push her away but* **RUBY** *clings on to her.*

You can't leave me too. I know I'm a nightmare, I say awful things, I'm disgusting and I stink, but please, please… I'll do better, I will.

JULIE Ruby.

RUBY Please, Julie. Please.

JULIE *peels* **RUBY** *off her and exits upstairs.*

RUBY *is left alone.*

Scene Four

Later the same evening.

The plated-up meals are on the dinner table and a bottle of wine.

GERRY *sits at the table, eating.* **JULIE** *is standing at the open window. She is wearing her new cardigan.*

GERRY Better?

JULIE Not really.

GERRY Breathe in through your mouth, it might take the edge off.

JULIE Then it's in my mouth.

GERRY Have I told you about my mate Pete?

JULIE No.

GERRY Policeman Pete. He's got prizes for ballroom dancing. Built like a tank.

JULIE I'd remember.

GERRY Well. He kept getting on the wrong side of his inspector, bollockings time and again. So this day he sneaks into his office – the inspector's – gets up on the desk and those panels in the ceiling… Pete opens one up and scatters in a bag of frozen prawns…

You're sure I haven't told you? I tell everyone.

JULIE I'm sure.

GERRY These prawns… Once they defrosted – absolutely stunk the place out. The inspector could not for the life of him work out where it was coming from.

JULIE What happened?

GERRY He found them eventually. Threw them out.

JULIE Right. Maybe don't go on Graham Norton with that anecdote.

GERRY I'm just saying. Could something have been left, fallen down somewhere, going off?

JULIE So you can smell it?

GERRY On and off. There's nothing now, though, it's fine.

She returns to the table and picks at her food.

JULIE I can't eat this. You finish yours, though.

GERRY Nah. Full up.

JULIE You've barely touched it, did you not like it?

GERRY There's only so much potato and broccoli a man can eat.

JULIE I offered you the pastry. And the mushrooms. I don't know why you couldn't just pick the chicken out.

GERRY It doesn't work like that.

Anyway, these ready meals are full of salt aren't they.

And. All the more room for those little cheesecakes you mentioned. They are suitable for vegetarians aren't they?

JULIE Totally.

JULIE *clears the plates away.*

GERRY I'll do that, you made it.

JULIE I heated it up.

GERRY Still.

JULIE It's fine.

Exit **JULIE** *to the kitchen.*

GERRY *retrieves the newspaper from the coffee table – turns to the crossword.*

Enter **JULIE**.

Cheesecakes now or wait?

GERRY Wait five minutes. You're a crossword fan?

JULIE No. Ruby.

GERRY She hasn't got very far.

JULIE She just fills in random letters and colours the squares in.

GERRY *(reading)* Five down. "Wheel corrosion consume". six letters.

Will she mind if I ...?

JULIE Probably. But you don't always get what you want. It will be a good life lesson for her.

GERRY I hope she doesn't feel like she has to stay in her room when I'm here.

JULIE We've had a falling out.

GERRY Anything I can help with?

JULIE No.

I'll get a pen.

GERRY No need. Always prepared.

GERRY *retrieves a small pencil like the ones you steal from IKEA. Also a pair of reading glasses.*

Puzzle Pencil and I have battled some difficult conundrums, let me tell you.

Crosswords. Dingbats, word searches. He's by my side every step of the way.

(To puzzle pencil) Do you know the answer, Puzzle Pencil?

"Yes I do, Gerry".

(To puzzle pencil) Then what are you waiting for, man?

(Filling in the answer) "Rotate".

JULIE You're a funny fish.

GERRY Am I?

JULIE A "right funny fish". Iris used to say that.

GERRY Is that your mum?

JULIE Yeah. She liked a good crossword too.

GERRY My mum'd kill me if I called her Joyce.

JULIE Why, is that not her name?

GERRY You don't talk about her, do you?

JULIE Why would I talk about your mam?

GERRY I understand. If it's too raw.

JULIE It's not "raw".

I used to call her Mam then I stopped.

GERRY Why?

JULIE I stopped being her daughter.

GERRY You never stop being someone's daughter.

JULIE I did.

GERRY Did she bring you up on her own?

JULIE Why does it matter?

GERRY Just wondering if you call your dad "Dad"?

JULIE I did. Till he buggered off. He was so young. Too young. They both were.

JULIE Do you like this cardigan?

GERRY What? Yes, it's nice and bright.

Four across. "A healthy source of water".

A source of water. Healthy. Four letters. Come on, it's easy.

JULIE "Well".

GERRY There you go.

Look at us, the dream team. I'll bring my slippers next time I come. There are few things better in life than slippers and a crossword.

GERRY *goes back to the crossword. But his words and the domestic scene are making* **JULIE** *uncomfortable. She takes the paper off* **GERRY**. *She goes to undo his trousers.*

You don't have to.

JULIE I want to.

GERRY Ruby.

JULIE Fuck her. She's sulking, she won't come down.

GERRY Thank you, but…

I've got an early start in the morning. I've got to be at Grinkle Park for nine…

JULIE You don't have to stay over, we can just…

GERRY Julie…really, thank you but…

JULIE Stop saying thank you.

If you really want me to stop, I'll stop.

GERRY …

JULIE *is on her knees.*

You've got grey in your roots.

JULIE And you've got a small cock, you don't hear me going on about it.

The moment ruined, **JULIE** *gets up.*

GERRY Sorry, I didn't mean… I just meant, I didn't know you dyed your hair.

It's a compliment really, that it looks so natural.

JULIE …

GERRY It's probably for the best. I think I've shagged myself dry. One night off, regroup – then I'll be right back on that horse. And this is nice too, isn't it. Cos I want there to be more to it. Conversation. Team work. Drinking some nice wine. Some wine.

It's a beautiful venue, Grinkle Park. Do you know it?

JULIE No.

GERRY As long as this weather holds I'll be able to get some great shots in the grounds.

JULIE What are you talking about?

GERRY I'm doing Monica and Steve's wedding photos tomorrow. I told you.

JULIE You didn't.

You told me about Policeman Pete and his shellfish…

GERRY Hey, Pete's not shellfish, he's a good bloke.

JULIE …

GERRY I do photography on the side. Have done for a couple of years, I'm quite in demand.

JULIE I can think of nothing worse. A stressed bride and groom. All those guests. Isn't it like trying to herd cats?

GERRY Not at all. I'm recording the best day of their lives for them to keep and remember, when it's all beginning.

Their joy gives me joy. You must get that too, when someone does their first three-point turn or passes their driving test.

JULIE Usually just a sense of horror that they're going to be let loose on the roads.

GERRY You taught them. Mind, I've been in a car with you.

JULIE Oi.

GERRY And it's the total opposite to the cleaning, isn't it. From going in, scrubbing away the worst time in someone's life. I couldn't do one without the other. They both keep me sane in their own way.

JULIE You're a dark horse, aren't you.

GERRY Am I?

A funny fish and a dark horse, eh.

Unnoticed by them, **RUBY** *appears on the stairs – listening.*

JULIE Look me in the eyes, Gerry.

GERRY What?

JULIE Come on, really look.

He does.

What do you see when you look at me?

GERRY I see someone gorgeous…

JULIE No, come on.

GERRY I see…you.

JULIE And what's that?

GERRY Julie.

Julie not Jules.

Who drinks white not red, tea not coffee. She's clever and gorgeous. With lovely hair –

JULIE No. Really, really look.

GERRY What do you want me to say?

JULIE I don't know.

It doesn't matter.

Exit **JULIE** *to the kitchen.*

GERRY Eyes don't see, you know.

The brain sees, eyes transmit. Matty told me. He's always reading stuff, coming out with facts. The light from an object, it goes in through the pupil and changes into electrical signals that go to the brain. It's the brain that sees colour, depth, movement – it uses what we've seen before, memories, emotions, to create the picture.

JULIE *returns with the mini cheesecakes on a plate.*

Clever stuff, isn't it.

Does Ruby's eye – lack of – does it affect her much, what she can see and do?

JULIE It's all she's ever known.

GERRY How did it happen?

Is that ok to ask?

JULIE It's not something we talk about.

RUBY I'll tell you.

JULIE How long have you been earwigging?

RUBY My ears were burning.

RUBY *comes down into the room.*

(Re the cheesecakes) Well aren't these adorable. Can I?

She packed me off to bed without any supper.

So, are you sitting comfortably? Once upon a time there was this little girl out on the beach with her mam.

JULIE Ruby.

RUBY He asked. I'm telling him.

GERRY You don't have to.

RUBY If you're not interested.

GERRY I am.

RUBY This little girl, she went running off and fell over.

JULIE Who says you went running off?

RUBY Can I get a word out?

Next thing Mam knew, I'd vanished. She looked around and there I was, face down in the sand. There was glass there. A shard stuck in my eye. The eye was removed. The end.

JULIE You make it sound like it was your fault.

RUBY She told me to keep a hold of her hand and I didn't.

JULIE You remember that?

RUBY No. She told me.

(To **GERRY***)* Mam wasn't blaming me.

RUBY Honesty. We should always be able to look ourselves in the eye.

JULIE Did you want something, or…?

RUBY Just nebbing.

I'll just… One for the road. *(She takes some more cheesecakes)*

Exit **RUBY** *back upstairs.*

GERRY She's a one, isn't she.

JULIE *(calling up to her)* I can still see you.

RUBY *(offstage)* Spoilsport.

JULIE I can't believe that's what Iris told her.

GERRY Is that not what happened?

JULIE To blame her.

JULIE When I was a kid, when I was naughty or I annoyed her – which was all the time – she'd make me stand there. You can even see where the carpet's worn. Do you know what it's like staring at yourself for ten minutes, twenty, an hour. You get very familiar with your flaws, with everything that's wrong with you.

There's no honesty, it's control. A human being would tell her it was an accident, but Iris. She wanted Ruby believing that if she's wilful, disobedient, then look what happens – she gets hurt. Best to be good, stay close, safe.

She's wrapped her up so tight in cotton wool…now look at the mess she's left behind.

GERRY Guilt.

JULIE What?

GERRY She couldn't stop Ruby's accident so she wanted to keep her from all future harm. It makes sense. She held her tighter. A mother's reaction, it's only natural.

JULIE Is that right?

Iris dying is the best thing that could happen to Ruby.

GERRY My cousin –

JULIE We're not talking about your cousin.

GERRY No. But he's an agoraphobic.

JULIE Ruby's not agoraphobic.

GERRY She couldn't go to her own mother's funeral.

JULIE You're not listening. She thinks she can't, without Iris –

GERRY Ok, but, my cousin, he went to a hypnotherapist, and he –

JULIE How did he manage that if he's agoraphobic?

GERRY Good point. The hypnotherapist came to him, then. A Paul McKenna type, you know, and he said –

JULIE I don't care what he said.

GERRY I just think…maybe she should see someone. My cousin –

JULIE You're such a Jonny Two Shits.

GERRY A what?

JULIE One-upping everything. "I had one shit, yeah well I had two".

GERRY Charming.

JULIE I'm sorry, are you calling me uncouth now?

GERRY No.

JULIE An uncouth, greying old trout. No wonder you don't want to shag me –

GERRY I do want to shag you.

JULIE But I'm so uncouth.

GERRY Jesus Christ this is exhausting.

JULIE I can't stand it. *(Goes back to the window for air)*

GERRY Can we just… Please.

I'm having a mini cheesecake.

JULIE OK.

GERRY Do you want one? Come and have a cheescake.

She does. They eat.

GERRY You've got a fan in Matty.

JULIE …

GERRY He's your number one fan.

JULIE Dear God, is he going to break my ankles with a sledgehammer?

GERRY Most people…they try but they're not actually engaging with him. They smile, tilt their heads, bless. But you – you really had a connection.

JULIE He's a nice lad.

GERRY He hasn't shut up about you.

JULIE I'm a novelty. I bought him that ice-cream.

GERRY He's not that easily won over.

JULIE He'll have forgotten about me by next week.

GERRY He won't. You've got a knack with him. He's a particular kid, not everyone can cope. Even his mum gets snappy with him –

JULIE Laura has him all the time, though –

GERRY Paula. I'd have him more if she let me.

Did he tell you his joke?

JULIE "Moo York Times"? Yes. More than once.

GERRY I bet you laughed each time, though.

You're a natural. It's such a shame…

JULIE What is?

GERRY You not having any kids. Was it Matthew, did he not want –

JULIE What kind of question is that?

GERRY I'm not being funny. It's not for everyone, I know, but. It's a real pity.

GERRY *goes to his coat, retrieves a child's drawing.*

He's done you a picture.

You're very honoured. Matty's pictures aren't for just anyone.

But **JULIE** *doesn't take it.*

That's you. Me. Him. Your epic sandcastle today. Dream team.

JULIE I didn't really do anything.

GERRY For a lad that spends all his time glued to his Xbox, I wouldn't have thought a bucket and spade would hold any delights, but he's already on at me to bring him back to build some more.

JULIE That'll be nice. A nice thing for the two of you.

GERRY Don't think you're getting out of it that easily. You're a large part of the appeal.

He proffers the pictures towards her again. She still doesn't take it.

He worked really hard on it.

JULIE He shouldn't of.

GERRY He wanted to.

JULIE You have it. Or Pauline.

GERRY Paula.

He did it for you.

JULIE I think this might not be…we're spending so much time together. I'll be heading home soon, so…

GERRY Have you set a date yet?

JULIE No. Soon.

GERRY I really like you, Julie.

JULIE You don't know me.

GERRY I do.

And, over time… I'm in this for the long haul.

He tries again with the picture –.

JULIE I don't want it. He shouldn't be getting attached, you shouldn't be encouraging him.

GERRY I'm not.

JULIE If I'd known you were bringing him today…

GERRY It's my Saturday. And he wanted to meet you, who Daddy's been telling him about.

JULIE I've not even known you a week. Shit. This isn't fair.

GERRY What isn't?

JULIE Putting me in this positon.

Letting him think I'm…in his life.

GERRY You are in his life.

JULIE Hardly.

GERRY You're in my life, you're in his.

JULIE You're the second person to say that to me today.

GERRY Well then.

You liked spending time with him, I saw you.

JULIE I was being polite.

GERRY He adores you.

JULIE I was tolerating him. He's hard work and clingy. And boring.

GERRY Don't say that.

JULIE He's boring and I was bored. But you gave me no choice so I let you drag me along to the bloody beach, I gritted my teeth and got through it. But it's not an experience I'm going to repeat, so…

Silence.

GERRY I take it back.

JULIE What's that?

GERRY That it's a pity you're childless.

JULIE "Childless".

GERRY You'd have to show compassion, kindness. How does someone, a woman – I mean, I'm not being funny – but a woman especially…

JULIE Go on.

GERRY Heartless.

JULIE Wow.

GERRY I don't know how else to describe it. Whatever's inside you. There's nothing soft, is there, nothing nurturing.

JULIE We can't all pop them out like Pauline.

GERRY Paula.

JULIE Just has to uncross her legs and whoops, there's twins in there.

GERRY That's what we are, though, isn't it? Survival of the species, a desire to reproduce.

JULIE Oh I had the desire, don't you worry.

GERRY Well something went wrong.

JULIE How many girls had you had sex with by the time you were twenty?

GERRY What?

JULIE Ballpark.

GERRY Not as many as I'd have liked.

JULIE I'd been through the whole school, sixth form, college –

Does that bother you?

GERRY No.

JULIE I wasn't doing it for fun. I liked it, let's be very clear on that. Are we clear?

GERRY Yes.

JULIE But there was a reason. A plan. When I was with those boys… I mattered, it mattered – what we were doing.

Look at your face.

GERRY What?

JULIE I was going to have a baby. Right from when I was tiny I had dolls, prams, all the little outfits. And that desire – it only got stronger as I grew up. This would be mine, for me. And I would get it right, not like Iris. She treated me like a dead weight, dragging her down, but *my* baby – there'd only be love. Love no matter what.

So stupid. So dangerous. But don't worry, us girls who shag around, we're whores not mothers. I got my punishment.

GERRY Punishment?

JULIE Chlamydia. I'd had it for years, apparently. Quietly wreaking havoc. I only found out when me and Matthew finally went to the doctors. Bunk-ups round the back of the chippie hadn't worked, but a respectable married woman – they have babies, it's what they do. Not me, though. Not fit for purpose.

GERRY …

JULIE Oh that shut you up.

GERRY I had no idea.

JULIE I'm less of an abomination of womanhood now it's "can't" not "won't". I am pleased.

GERRY I'm sorry. I just get so…where Matty's concerned… family…

JULIE I'm not your family.

GERRY You could be, though.

JULIE What?

GERRY Don't you think, rather than pushing us away…

I can give you what you want.

JULIE And what's that?

GERRY I see you now, Julie. When you asked me before to look into your eyes. You wanted me to see all the love in you. And I do, I see it now. And I can return that love. Matty can.

This is your chance.

JULIE I had my chance.

GERRY You told me all that for a reason.

JULIE I tell everyone. People at bus stops.

GERRY No.

We can be a family.

All those years of wanting, don't mess it up for yourself again.

Imagine it – his sweet face smiling up at you, his laughter. All that love, love no matter what.

You can be a real woman. A mother.

JULIE Fuck off, Gerry. Your retard son has a mother. He's your family, your problem, don't try and drag me down with you.

Exit **GERRY**.

(Shouting after him) And there was pork gelatine in those mini cheesecakes, so fuck you.

JULIE *goes to "the spot", trying to look at herself in the mirrors but she can't.*

She tries to take a mirror down but it refuses to come away from the wall. She gets increasingly angry, eventually wrenching it off. It drops and breaks. She yells in frustration.

RUBY *appears on the stairs in bare feet.*

RUBY What's happening?

JULIE Go back upstairs.

RUBY Where's Gerry?

JULIE Fuck me, what is that fucking stench?

You must be able to smell it?

RUBY Maybe something…

JULIE Has something fallen down somewhere, going off…

RUBY *pads around the room, searching.* **JULIE** *looks too.* **RUBY** *ends up by the post pile.*

RUBY Here. I can smell it here.

JULIE *comes over. She picks up the parcel, sniffs it and recoils – clearly they have found the source.*

She carries it to the coffee table. Reads the address label.

JULIE Bloody hell Iris, what have you been ordering?

RUBY What is it?

JULIE *opens the parcel, releasing waves of smell.*

Christ…

The outer packaging reveals a cardboard box. She opens it and pulls out some packing foam.

JULIE Urghhh.

RUBY What?

JULIE It's all wet inside.

Get a cloth, will you.

Ruby.

RUBY I'm going to throw up.

RUBY *runs back upstairs.*

JULIE *pulls out a glass jar – through cloudy liquid we can see there is an eyeball floating inside. She peers at it –.*

JULIE Jesus, fuck.

End of Act One

ACT TWO

Scene One

JULIE The room is hot with the smell. Blood. Raw meat. Sweat. It's thick and strong, seeping into the walls and the metal bed frame and the sheets.

The noise fills up the whole space. Even when it's just her breathing, low and long, or short sharp gasps, it's coming from somewhere else inside her. From all of her. Her body knows that this is what she is built for.

I'm backed into a corner. My ears are full, my nose, while my eyes sting and stream. I daren't blink in case I miss a moment of it. I've missed so much already, each flutter, kick, but no more.

Then… I don't know what's happening, a flurry of voices, movement, gloved hands and red flesh…and now suddenly it's over, it's done, and I'm a beat behind everyone else.

The midwife lies you on her chest. Skin on skin. You curl around to fit the shape of her. Instinct. I see her see you. There is no gap, no join. You're hers. From her. You are one.

Time passes. I'm a spectator. They bring her strong tea and buttered toast. It wafts over, I'm starving for it, but no toast for me. I haven't done anything.

Then, finally, I'm invited to join in. You're quiet now, wrapped up tight, passed over carefully. I can't find a curve for you to fit into. I hold you slightly away.

Your eyes are closed but I can feel hers on me. When I glance over she shuts them tight but I know she's watching, checking. Of course she is. She's lying there; torn open and emptied while I sit comfortably with the spoils.

I look and look but I can't see you. A mass in a blanket, fat face all blotchy, nose, eyes, lips. I can make out the parts, but not the whole. How long have I wanted to hold you? I wait for it to overwhelm me, for the rush…

I close my eyes. They're so dry I feel the eyelids scrape down. Relief. You're heavier than I thought you'd be. I hear my own breath in my ears. Maybe it'll be ok.

You start crying. My eyes snap awake, wild, staring into your black, open mouth.

It wasn't meant to be like this.

Scene Two

The next day – morning.

The empty frame of the broken mirror is propped against the wall.

GERRY*'s camera is on the dining table.*

On the coffee table are two mugs of tea and a wad of bloody tissues.

RUBY *is on the settee in her dressing gown. One of her feet has plasters on it.*

GERRY *is staring at the carpet, carrying a plastic carrier bag full of the broken mirrors bits. He is dressed in a smart suit.*

GERRY I think I've got it all but be careful.

Hang on…

He spies a tiny shard of glass from the mirror –.

Gotcha.

He drops it in the carrier bag.

He retrieves his mug of tea.

How you feeling?

RUBY Fine.

GERRY How's your foot?

RUBY Also fine.

GERRY I'll have this then do a once around with the hoover.

RUBY You've lost a button.

GERRY Damn. This was new out the packet this morning.

RUBY Was it a nice wedding?

GERRY I'd barely got set up when you rang.

I got a few shots of the bride getting ready. Do you want to see?

GERRY *shows her the camera screen.*

You can see them better on here.

That's Monica, the bride.

Her mother.

Monica again. If I crop that one right down, get a nice filter on it.

Maid of honour. She was a one. I thought she was going to swing for me when I said I had to leave.

RUBY What did you tell them?

GERRY Family emergency.

I left them with Shaun, my second shooter. It'll give him a chance to use his new seventy-two hundred he's been banging on about.

RUBY These are quite good. For you.

GERRY Thanks.

RUBY Mam never took photos. She said they're fake. Frozen. All that "smile for the camera". She preferred the mirrors – in the moment, as you are. Even if you don't like what you see.

Julie hates them. She won't look in them.

GERRY I know.

RUBY She's like an island, won't look at herself, barely looks at me. She doesn't come near me.

GERRY We all grieve in different ways.

RUBY She's never liked me. Me or Mam.

GERRY I'm sure she does.

RUBY She goes on and on at me, but she's got no idea. People stare out there, whisper. Call me names.

GERRY That says more about them than you.

RUBY You sound like Mam.

GERRY Have you never wanted to get a prosthesis?

RUBY Oh. So, don't care about what other people think but you should get yourself normal looking.

GERRY I didn't say that.

RUBY We tried false eyes growing up. One plopped out during a swimming lesson, floated off down the shallow end.

GERRY Your face would still be growing, changing. But now you're older.

RUBY When they first removed my eye in the hospital, I had to have this plastic shell in the socket to keep the shape while it healed. I don't remember it, Mam told me, how I screamed the place down when they stitched my eyelid together to keep it in.

GERRY The ones you get now, though, they're custom-made, low maintenance. You just give them a rinse to keep them clean.

RUBY Aren't you the expert.

GERRY We looked it up, me and Matty.

RUBY You've told him about me?

GERRY Of course. Matty always like to hear about new people, learn new things. We both do.

RUBY You're a funny fish.

GERRY So I've been told.

Do you want to tell me what you and Julie have fallen out about?

RUBY Who says we've fallen out?

GERRY The names you've been calling her.

Where is she?

RUBY I thought she'd come straight back. A quick walk round the block but… All night. That's a long fucking walk.

GERRY She's been out all night?

RUBY Yeah. And I sat up all night. I was ringing and ringing her till I realised she'd left her phone.

GERRY Her car's still there.

RUBY She left her keys. Everything, bag, purse.

GERRY Can you think of anywhere she might have gone?

RUBY No. I thought she might be with you.

GERRY I've not seen her since last night. We had a bit of a row.

I should look for her. She can't be far.

RUBY You can't leave me as well.

GERRY Has she done this before?

RUBY Yeah. With you.

She's alright, isn't she?

GERRY Course. She's fine.

RUBY She'll be shacked up with someone else, probably.

GERRY Yeah.

GERRY *takes a big gulp of tea – he starts to cough.*

RUBY You ok?

GERRY …down the wrong way.

RUBY *hits him on the back.*

RUBY Do you need the Heimlich Manoeuvre?

GERRY I'm fine. It was just a sip of tea.

RUBY I wouldn't know how to do it anyway. Not properly. Do you?

GERRY Yes. I've done first aid classes.

RUBY Do you know the Recovery Position?

GERRY Yes.

RUBY Do it on me.

GERRY Why?

RUBY Show me on me, what to do.

RUBY *is already getting down on the floor.*

Come on.

GERRY *carefully moves* **RUBY** *into the recovery position.*

GERRY This arm at a right angle…

This one across the chest…

Leg up…roll on to your side…

Lift the chin.

There. Consider yourself recovered.

Silence.

RUBY *just lies there.* **GERRY** *isn't sure what to do for the best. Eventually –.*

RUBY Mam fell there.

Her skirt was twisted. She was on her front.

GERRY What happened?

RUBY Has Julie never said?

GERRY No.

RUBY Something burst in her brain.

She was standing there, we were laughing – she had a brilliant laugh – then she sort of fluttered down.

RUBY I ran over to her. I was straight there, but her eyes were already closed.

GERRY I'm sorry.

RUBY Are your parents still alive?

GERRY Yes.

RUBY What's their names?

GERRY Joyce and Jon. Without an "h".

RUBY You should ring Joyce, ring her right now, tell her you love her. I wish I could have mam back for an extra minute, thirty seconds, so I could tell her once more.

GERRY I'm sure she knew.

RUBY But I'm totally alone now, floating free.

GERRY You've got Julie.

RUBY Hollow fucking laughter.

GERRY Is your dad not around? Can't he help?

RUBY He died before I was born, car accident.

GERRY I'm sorry.

RUBY At least with a car crash, though, it's an event, isn't it. It's urgent and loud.

But Mam. Not a whisper as she crumpled.

I put her in the Recovery Position. What I thought it was.

She looked peaceful. Even with me manhandling her, getting it wrong, she didn't looked scared or in pain.

GERRY That's good.

RUBY What's the worst thing you've ever seen? At your work, there must be some horror shows.

GERRY There can be.

Nobody likes getting an unattended death.

RUBY Unattended. For how long?

GERRY Depends. Weeks, sometimes months, sometimes longer.

RUBY There's nobody to know they've died?

GERRY No.

RUBY That'll be me.

I'll be left decaying for months, years, no-one to notice or come looking.

GERRY Don't be a dafty.

RUBY Julie's going to leave me here on my own. The neighbours will only call the police when the smell gets too bad, by then I'll be putrid and you'll have to come and scrub me out of the floorboards.

GERRY We've got a tool for that.

RUBY Really?

GERRY Yeah. And pliers for picking bits of skull out of walls. Brain dries hard like cement, so we use a putty knife to scrape it up.

And blood, it congeals into jelly after a couple of hours, so we shovel it into bags.

RUBY I did not know that.

GERRY Good. You should have no reason to.

Let's find your Julie, eh. Get up. Come on.

RUBY She ran off because of the parcel.

GERRY What parcel?

RUBY It's out the back. I didn't know what to… I put it outside.

Exit **GERRY** *to the kitchen.*

He returns with the cardboard box and a thick manila envelope. He puts them on the coffee table.

GERRY Can I?

RUBY *nods. She is backed away as far as she can be.*

He opens the box and pulls out the glass jar. He studies it. He is calm.

That's an eyeball.

RUBY There's the other one too. Its jar broke. Rotten and…urgh.

GERRY *looks in the box.*

GERRY That's what the smell is, then.

RUBY *(the envelope)* They were in with them.

GERRY *(pulls out documents – scans)* Have you been through this?

RUBY A bit.

GERRY Iris has left you her eyeballs.

Did Julie read it?

RUBY S'pose. The envelope was open when I came down from throwing up.

GERRY It'll have been a shock for her.

RUBY I'm not exactly taking it in my stride.

GERRY Letters from a solicitor. Doctor. The coroner, the medical facility.

RUBY Yes.

GERRY Well she's certainly dotted the tees and crossed the – sorry.

RUBY Why aren't you freaking out?

GERRY I've seen worse things at work. This is all rather civilised.

RUBY It's fucked up.

GERRY People leave their loved ones things. My nana left me her china dogs. Your mum bequeathed you her eyes.

RUBY What are you doing?

GERRY *exits to the kitchen with the box.*

GERRY Getting rid of this.

RUBY Getting rid how?

GERRY I'll think of something. But it's a mess…

RUBY *keeps her distance but stares at the glass jar on the table.*

Enter **GERRY**.

(Picking up the jar) That is quite something.

It's so green. Did her eyes look that green when she was alive?

RUBY It was addressed *to* Iris. Is that someone's idea of a joke?

I don't remember it arriving. Julie must have signed for it. We've just been piling her post up on top of it.

GERRY Eyes are the least donated organ, you know. Windows to the soul, and all that. Iris's whole life went through this. She's gifted that to you. It's incredible.

From the first thing she ever saw right to the last. To you, laughing.

RUBY *is overcome with emotion – trying (failing) to hold it in. A brief burst of pent-up grief. It subsides.*

Can I take your photo?

RUBY Piss off.

GERRY Please.

RUBY No.

GERRY Let you see what she saw. The last thing.

RUBY I know what she saw. I can look at it anytime I like. I live in a house of fucking mirrors.

She was always watching me, but all she ever saw is what isn't there.

Mam did take photos. There are albums of baby pictures up there. Then it stops.

Nothing.

GERRY You are beautiful, Ruby.

RUBY You're in an exclusive group of one who thinks so.

GERRY No. How you see yourself in these is different to how anyone else sees you. And none of them will see you the same. A photo, though. You can take a step back. Yes it's frozen, a moment, but it might be a really great moment caught forever.

RUBY Have you got your camera ready?

GERRY Yes.

RUBY I won't say "cheese".

GERRY You don't have to.

A decision. **RUBY** *pulls the eye patch off and faces* **GERRY** *full face on.*

He takes her photo.

Scene Three

Same day – later.

The jar is on the coffee table.

GERRY *is holding an official-looking letter from out of the manila envelope – he is on his mobile whilst generously spraying Febreze around.*

GERRY *(on the phone)* I appreciate that…no, absolutely. If you can just read that back to me one more time… no, no, it's WF…no "F"… "F" for Freddy… Yes… K9WF/66577881…eight-one, that's right…no problem…

Enter **RUBY** *from upstairs. She is out of the dressing gown and dressed in clean clothes, socks and slippers. She is drying her damp hair with a towel.*

She carries a printed-out photo, a photo album and a sewing box.

She sees him on the phone –.

RUBY Julie?

GERRY No.

(On phone) Ok… Ok…well if you could…as soon as possible. Ok. Bye…thank you, bye. *(Hangs up)*

RUBY Who was it?

GERRY This medical place…thought I'd make myself useful.

They're going to get a manager to ring me back.

RUBY Did you give them hell?

GERRY I'll save it for someone who can do something. Then I'll let loose the fireworks.

Do you feel better for that?

RUBY Much.

GERRY Did you leave the conditioner in like I said?

RUBY Yes. Smell.

She holds her hair out for him to sniff. He does.

GERRY Minty fresh.

I've put a wash on. And it's starting to smell better in here, I think you'll agree.

(The spray) This was in the cupboard. Better than an air freshener. It eats the odour rather than masks it.

Smell.

RUBY Barely a trace of decomposition.

GERRY I've also given a couple of the lads a ring.

RUBY What lads?

GERRY Police. I know them through work. There's been no accidents or incidents involving anyone matching Julie's description.

RUBY Course not.

GERRY Is that the photo?

RUBY It looks different printed off.

Do you like it?

GERRY Do you?

RUBY That's not what I look like in my head.

GERRY What do you look like?

RUBY Dunno.

(Re her eye patch) I always think that without this…that it's holding me together or… I don't know. But this girl…there's strength here, an energy…

GERRY This girl is you.

RUBY Can I keep this?

GERRY Course.

RUBY I'll put it in here. *(The photo album)*

I thought you might want to see. Prove I was cute once.

GERRY You're cute now.

GERRY *flips through the photos.*

Don't your mum and Julie look alike.

RUBY No.

GERRY They do.

RUBY *(re the sewing box)* I thought you might want to fix your shirt.

It's Mam's, there's all different buttons. Just use what you need.

GERRY Thank you.

RUBY Go on, then.

GERRY *picks out a button and a thread/needle.*

He is trying to sew the button on while still wearing the shirt.

What you doing? Take it off.

GERRY *takes his shirt off. Sews.*

RUBY *sits alongside him.*

Will you show me how?

GERRY You've never sewn a button on?

RUBY No.

GERRY It's easy. I've double-threaded the needle –

She gets closer.

Just hold the button in place, through and then back down the opposite hole

RUBY I can't see.

She gets closer.

GERRY Through and through. Through and through.

Silence. **GERRY** *sews.*

Eventually –.

RUBY Isn't it funny how quickly you get used to stuff.

GERRY Like what?

RUBY Like, Mam's eye on the coffee table.

Like, you being here.

GERRY …

RUBY Will you stroke my hair?

It's minty fresh, you said so.

GERRY *sort of pats her head.*

No. The length of it down, like a cat.

He does once.

Keep going.

Really press down so I can feel it.

Mam would do it for ages. Hours and hours.

All is still and quiet.

The doorbell rings.

GERRY *gets up, pulls his shirt on.*

Don't stop.

GERRY It might be Julie.

RUBY Make her wait.

GERRY *opens the door.*

JULIE *is dressed in the same clothes as last time we saw her. She has slept in them, been out all night. She looks rough. She pushes straight in past* **GERRY.**

Whatever tat you're selling we don't want any.

JULIE *heads upstairs.*

(Calling after her) Oi, I'm talking to you… Oi.

JULIE …

RUBY *(to* **GERRY***)* Sit down.

GERRY She's upset.

RUBY I'm upset.

Sit down.

GERRY *(re the carpet)* There's…erm…

JULIE *has traipsed dog shit in to the house.*

RUBY Jesus.

GERRY I'll get a cloth.

Exit **GERRY** *to the kitchen.*

JULIE *appears from upstairs dragging her case with her.*

RUBY You. Look at this.

This. What you've walked right though.

JULIE Shit.

RUBY Shit is right. You need to clean that up. Disgusting.

JULIE Can I get by, please.

JULIE has her handbag – is getting her things together, phone, checking her purse, etc.

Enter GERRY with a cloth and a bowl of water –.

GERRY Is this cloth ok to use?

RUBY What are you doing?

JULIE Going.

GERRY Where?

JULIE Home.

I've stayed too long already. It was never long-term, you know that.

JULIE pulls some money out of her purse. Leaves it on the table. She hesitates by the jar, but that is all.

She picks her handbag up to leave – the strap comes loose. Everything falls out on to the shitty carpet.

Fuck's sake.

She gingerly tries to pick the things up. The movement, the shit, a hangover are making her nauseous. Is she going to throw up?

Jesus, what does he feed that dog?

RUBY Are you hungover? I can smell it on you. And fags. Through the shit.

I told you that's what she was doing last night. Living it up, getting some bloke to buy her drinks for her.

. . .

She's not denying it.

GERRY Where did you go?

JULIE Places. The beach.

GERRY Where did you stay?

RUBY He means in whose bed?

JULIE I slept on a bench on the promenade.

GERRY Bloody hell, Julie.

GERRY'*s phone rings. He retrieves it.*

GERRY It's the medical place. I need to take this.

Exit **GERRY** *to the kitchen.*

JULIE What's he doing here?

RUBY I rang him

JULIE Why?

RUBY Who else was there? You fucked off without a backwards glance. He answered first ring, thinking it was you. He dropped everything. He's tidied it all up. Febrezed the place within an inch of its life. It eats the odour rather than masks it. He'll have to clean around again now, thanks to you, shitty shoes.

JULIE ...

RUBY Are you even going to mention it?

I had a heart attack when I saw what was in there. That you just left for me to find. The smell alone made me sick, actually sick, so when I saw it ...

On my own, no idea where you'd gone–

JULIE Shut up.

RUBY What?

JULIE I don't want to hear it. Your voice, on and on... When do you ever even breathe?

Enter **GERRY.**

GERRY It's like trying to reason with a toaster. They've got their script, not budging.

They take no responsibility for any damage caused in transit.

And the address label – why is it addressed "to" Iris? "Unfortunate human error". You can make a complaint in writing within twenty eight days.

JULIE Did they say what we're meant to do with the other one?

GERRY They won't take it back so…

JULIE So, what?

GERRY I don't know. That was it.

JULIE What have you done with it?

RUBY Gerry dealt with it.

JULIE Where is it?

RUBY He sorted it.

He's been amazing.

GERRY I put it in the freezer.

JULIE …

Exit **JULIE** *to the kitchen.*

GERRY I didn't want to throw it out. Seemed disrespectful.

Enter **JULIE**.

She brings a freezer bag with a frozen eyeball inside.

JULIE Are you kidding me?

GERRY It was spoiled, leaking. It seemed like the best thing.

JULIE You haven't even put a sticky label on it.

GERRY Saying what?

JULIE I don't know, some warning.

RUBY "Chicken", "mincemeat", "eyeball".

Aw Gerry, you're a dafty aren't you.

Give her here, Julie.

Julie.

JULIE Why?

RUBY Because she's mine.

JULIE Yours?

Does that make that one mine? *(The jar)*

RUBY She left them both for me. Because she loved me. It's an incredible gift. Gerry said.

JULIE It's pyschotic.

RUBY Put her back, she's melting.

GERRY I'll take it.

Exit **GERRY** *to the kitchen with the frozen eyeball.*

JULIE *gets her final things together.*

Goes to exit outside –.

JULIE It's the best thing. You'll be ok. When you need money, I'll transfer it.

I'll ring you.

RUBY No you won't.

You don't need to bother, anyway. Gerry's going to look after me.

JULIE What?

RUBY He's going to take care of me.

He's moving in.

Enter **GERRY**.

RUBY You are, aren't you?

GERRY What?

RUBY Moving in.

GERRY Am I?

RUBY So we're fine without you. Better even.

And Joyce and Jon – they'll come over for Sunday dinner. We'll have lamb. Matty can stay over. He can have your room.

GERRY Ruby, I never said –

RUBY He thinks I'm beautiful.

JULIE Is that right?

RUBY This face, as it is, the one you can't stomach.

He patched me up when you just left me. He was so tender, so careful.

A great big shard in my foot from the mirror you smashed.

I think he's got it all. It's in here. *(The carrier bag)*

We're going to bury it in the back garden. The broken mirror bits. Bury them like the Romans believed. It was the Romans?

GERRY Yes.

RUBY Under the tree during a full moon to stop the bad luck.

We are, aren't we Gerry.

Tell her.

Tell her, Gerry, how it's going to be.

She grabs him – kisses him.

GERRY *pushes her away, hard. Harder than he means to.*

JULIE Don't push her.

GERRY I'm sorry, I didn't mean to...

I should never have come back here.

JULIE Then why did you?

GERRY I thought you needed help. I thought I could help you.

JULIE Nobody asked for your help.

GERRY She did. Rang up in a right state. I walked out on a job to be here and this is what I get for it? You haven't even said thank you.

I am a nice person. Loyal, kind. I hold doors open, pay compliments even when they're not deserved. That cardigan, for example.

I'm helping. So why I am always the one left cleaning up the shit?

Beat.

RUBY Do you love me?

JULIE Ruby, enough.

RUBY Not him, you. Do you love me?

JULIE *opens the front door.*

Do you, though?

Julie.

Julie.

Do you love me?

JULIE No.

I can't. I can't let myself…

RUBY Look at me.

Julie.

GERRY Julie.

JULIE looks. RUBY is holding a shard of the mirror on her wrist.

RUBY I will. I will.

JULIE Go on then.

GERRY No.

JULIE Go on. Do it. You are so pathetic, Ruby. And weak. No wonder Iris dropped dead, putting up with this.

RUBY Can I tell you something about me, Gerry?

GERRY Yes.

RUBY About my accident. The most important thing that ever happened to me, that she can never be bothered to even ask about.

JULIE Ruby –

RUBY I'm not talking to you, I'm talking to Gerry. Gerry who said I was beautiful. You did, didn't you?

GERRY Yes.

RUBY I remember…not remember, but… I get flashes, things I saw just after I fell.

GERRY Go on.

RUBY My eye was a hard shell that cracked open when I landed, shattered into tiny shards that splintered out of the socket.

The pieces were so small and light they didn't sink into the sand but rested on top, and I could still see what they were seeing. I saw silver light glistening on the sea, the sun dazzling in the blue sky, bright yellow sand and a big painted sign for "Ices".

A couple of the shards landed facing me so I saw me lying there too – I was looking at me lying there. Behind me, the sky was falling in. That's the last thing my broken eye saw before it all went black.

Do you believe me?

GERRY Yes.

RUBY No you don't.

GERRY People believe all sorts of things. The Victorians – I saw this programme – they believed that the last thing a person saw was saved on their retina.

RUBY Really?

GERRY Yeah. The police would photograph the eyes of murder victims to try and see their killer there.

It might still be on catch-up, we can watch it now if you like, just give me the glass.

RUBY *(she doesn't)* Are you...are you saying the last thing that Mam saw is imprinted on there, preserved forever?

The fact that she was all alone.

GERRY She wasn't alone, you were with her.

RUBY No. I wasn't.

We'd argued, I was in my room.

No-one saw her fall like no-one saw me fall. I know how awful that is, to be scared and alone. Cos those shards of my eye, they never saw a person. No-one looking, no-one coming to help. The most important event of our lives, the moment everything changed. They went unwitnessed. And that's not right, it's not fair.

GERRY Tell her it's ok. Julie.

JULIE I can't.

RUBY She's not even listening.

GERRY Do something.

JULIE Like what?

GERRY Anything.

JULIE I can't. I can't do this...

JULIE *goes to exit.*

RUBY Julie.

GERRY Shit.

RUBY *is bleeding from her wrist.*

GERRY *dashes to* **RUBY**. **JULIE** *is frozen.*

Get that towel. There.

JULIE *does. She takes it to* **RUBY** *and holds it to her wrist.* **GERRY** *retrieves his phone.*

GERRY Hold it on. Hard.

RUBY Were you watching?

JULIE It's pouring right through.

GERRY *(on the phone)* Ambulance please.

RUBY Did you see?

JULIE Shhh. You're ok.

RUBY Did you see?

JULIE Yes. I saw. I saw you.

Scene Four

The very early hours of the following morning. It is still dark out.

The lights are on but the room is empty.

Things have been tidied away / piled up.

We hear keys in the front door.

Enter **JULIE**.

She still has **RUBY***'s dry blood on her clothes.*

She takes in the room.

Suddenly, enter **GERRY** *from the kitchen. He is in his crime scene biohazard coverall and face mask. He has his clean-up kit.* **JULIE** *gets a fright –.*

JULIE Bloody hell

GERRY Sorry. It's me, sorry.

I didn't hear you come in.

JULIE What are you doing?

GERRY I went home and got my kit.

I thought it was something useful I could do. Help.

JULIE Go home, Gerry.

GERRY Help me, I mean. Paula's applying for full custody. She's got Richard, the twins. She wants to move away, be a family.

JULIE Can she do that?

GERRY She's his mum. Mum trumps all.

So it's either this, with you, or back to nights on the sofa getting quietly obliterated while I wait for them to set a court date.

JULIE …

GERRY *(re the carpet)* It's come out really well. It won't stain, it hadn't dried in. It won't have seeped though, either, so no need to take the carpet up.

A thumbnail patch of blood on a carpet, there could be a two-foot wide stain on the floorboards underneath.

JULIE It's like a horror film – blood, shit, eyeballs. The place needs to be razed to the ground, not a once-around with some Shake n' Vac.

GERRY It's not Shake n' Vac.

It's industrial strength. You can't buy it in a shop. I'm trained, I've got certificates.

JULIE I know.

Silence.

GERRY Is she ok?

JULIE Yeah.

GERRY Sorry, I should have asked that the minute you walked in.

JULIE They're keeping her in. They've stitched her up but they want to check there's no nerve damage. She'll see a plastic surgeon tomorrow.

GERRY She's in the best place.

JULIE What you did…the towel, and…they said it was all the right things. I was useless, but you…

Thank you.

GERRY You're welcome.

Silence.

JULIE *looks through the neat piles of paperwork* **GERRY** *has amassed on the table.*

Legal. Medical. Administrative. Other.

She was very thorough, your mum. Everything primed and ready to go in the event of her death.

JULIE So it seems.

Where do you even start finding someone to do this?

GERRY You can find anyone to do anything these days.

JULIE But this is proper. Science, people in lab coats.

All that delay with the body. Her stipulating a closed coffin…

Shit. What do you think we buried? Do you think we buried anything? What if she's frozen in a chamber somewhere? Left instructions to post bits of herself back to us every few weeks.

GERRY I doubt it.

JULIE I wouldn't put it past her. Fingers by FedEx.

GERRY Pancreas by Parcel Force. Torso from TNT.

JULIE Yeah, ok.

GERRY Sorry, I thought we were… Sorry.

JULIE *looks though the photo album.*

JULIE Where did this come from?

GERRY Ruby brought it down to show me.

I took this one. I took most of them, but this one… The height of summer, no idea why Iris had that stupid furry hat out. But Ruby, she loved the feel of the fur on her belly. You can see. Grinning at each other, their faces splitting with those smiles.

GERRY *pulls out his photo of* **RUBY**.

GERRY I took this one.

JULIE Look at her.

What have we done to her?

GERRY There's strength. There's energy. She said so herself.

JULIE Did she?

JULIE *tears the photo down the middle, discards* **RUBY***'s "bad" side.*

A split second and it changed everything. Ruined. Her lovely, perfect face.

GERRY She's still a very striking young woman.

JULIE Then imagine what she could have been.

I need a drink.

GERRY There isn't any.

JULIE There's a cupboard full.

GERRY I tipped it all out.

JULIE Sorry, that sounded like "I tipped it all out".

GERRY Yes.

I don't really know why… I just thought, it's a slippery slope. In times of stress.

I'll replace it.

JULIE You will, yeah.

GERRY I can do you a cup of tea.

JULIE No.

GERRY Coffee?

JULIE No.

GERRY Water? You need to keep your fluids up.

JULIE I'm fine.

GERRY You're really not. Here, sit down.

JULIE No. Get off. Stand over there. Further.

I just… Don't be nice to me and I'll be fine.

Silence. Eventually –.

GERRY Soak it overnight, some Vanish in the machine and it'll come out like new.

JULIE What?

GERRY Your… *(The blood on her clothes).*

JULIE Shit.

Where's my case?

She pulls her cardigan and t-shirt off.

GERRY *retrieves her suitcase. She opens it, jumping back in fright finding the jar inside.*

GERRY Oh yeah, sorry, I put the… Iris in…

I didn't want her to get knocked.

JULIE *examines the jar closely.*

JULIE Doesn't it look weird out of your head. Have you seen how bright the colour is, that green.

My eyes are brown. And Ruby's.

GERRY Where do you think you'll put her?

JULIE I thought maybe on the mantelpiece.

Make a real feature out of it.

GERRY Oh.

JULIE Look at that glare. No-one looks at me like she did. And just when I think it's over, she has them plucked, pickled and posted.

JULIE *pulls on a fresh top.*

Ruby's right, she will have left them to her.

GERRY There's nothing in the paperwork about one or the other.

JULIE To watch over her. She wouldn't trust me with her, never did. Quite right too.

(To the jar) Or were you just wanting to stick around and watch me fuck up? Just like the old days eh. And now, I've put her back in a hospital bed.

Oi, look at me when I'm talking to you. The least you can do is look me in the eye…

The eye is bobbing around in the jar. **JULIE** *is being very rough with it – might drop it.*

GERRY *(intervening)* Careful. Julie.

JULIE Have it. I don't want it.

GERRY Are you ok?

(Re folding the stained clothes back into the suitcase) What am I doing, I don't want these. *(Re the cardigan)* Any use? You can cut it up for cleaning rags?

GERRY No thank you.

She zips up the case, takes it to the door.

You can't leave.

JULIE But that's what I do.

GERRY What about Ruby?

JULIE Did you hear her ask me if I love her?

GERRY Yes.

JULIE So you heard my answer. That I don't love her.

GERRY You said you can't let yourself love her.

JULIE Same thing.

GERRY Not at all.

JULIE "A mother is a woman in relation to a child to whom she has given birth." That's the definition. You can check if you like but it's right, I've looked it up.

GERRY I believe you.

JULIE There's so much stock in the action of giving birth. The ability to do that, it holds so much power. "Mum trumps all", your words. Paula can take your son away because she pushed him out of a hole the size of a peach. She wins.

GERRY Nothing's decided.

JULIE All I remember from watching Ruby's birth is the smell and the noise. It was disgusting.

Not hearts and flowers, no love rushing at me.

I waited for that instinct to kick in, but I was just playing pretend like I'd done with my dolls. Only they didn't struggle to writhe away from me, they stopped crying when I soothed them.

You don't get it, do you.

Iris had Ruby for me.

My egg, Matthew's sperm. Iris carried her because I couldn't.

GERRY …

JULIE It sounds so simple, doesn't it. She'd have her, I'd raise her, and the world would keep on turning. But it didn't.

And it came to a big, fat, juddering halt that day on the beach.

When I rang Iris from the hospital…she didn't even get angry.

She sat like a statue in the waiting room. I picked at a thread on my top until I put a hole in it.

Eventually a nurse appeared. "Are you Ruby's mother?". I paused. As long as it takes to breathe in to reply. Longer.

Then a voice next to me. "I am," says Iris. Quietly. Absolute conviction. The nurse didn't bat an eyelid, turned on her heels, but Iris stayed back. "Go home, look in the mirror, and if you can look yourself in the eye then come back." And off she went through the double doors to Ruby and the doctors. I stayed until I couldn't hear the squeak of her shoes anymore, I put my coat on and went home.

I packed my stuff and left.

GERRY You just gave her to her?

JULIE There was no paperwork. Iris's name was on the birth certificate.

I send money every month.

GERRY I not talking about the admin.

JULIE I know.

She wasn't ever mine to give.

When Iris was with Ruby there was gentleness, patience. Love that she never had for me. Ruby made Iris a mother. I watched it happen.

GERRY What was Matthew doing in all this?

JULIE I told him to bugger off before the second scan. He was in the way, fretting, freaking out. He'd done what I needed him for.

When they first told us that I couldn't…he was the one who asked about surrogacy. You had to be married, you had to use a friend or family.

We asked his sister but she said no. I asked a girl in the office where I worked. She moved desks. It was Iris or nothing. I begged, no self-respect. I flattered, cajoled, told her what a shit parent she was and she fucking owed me. Then, eventually, "yeah, ok" and we were off – tests, scans, needles. It took first go. That never happens. They kept warning us, the percentages, her age. But there it was.

Those nine months… I moved back in here and we were so close, me and Iris. We had something in common at last, something we were doing together. I really thought we'd be ok.

A nurse came along tonight. He said, "are you Ruby's mother?"

GERRY What did you say?

JULIE He took me through to her, those double doors, my shoes squeaking on the floor. When I saw her lying there…

It's so much harder if I let myself love her.

GERRY Let it be hard.

JULIE I tried.

GERRY Try again.

JULIE I kept waiting for Iris to appear, to take over. But I realised tonight, she's gone. It's on me now, and I felt… I don't know what, but the stirrings of something – not strong – but something…

GERRY Something good?

JULIE Something great. And really fucking terrifying.

GERRY That's good, isn't it.

JULIE Is it?

GERRY Don't you want her to see you for who you are?

JULIE I don't know what that is.

GERRY Her mother.

JULIE No.

There's so much…too much…

What if she doesn't like what she sees?

GERRY At least she knows what she's looking at.

Silence.

GERRY *gets up, retrieves his coat.*

JULIE At last, he runs for the hills.

GERRY Not quite. The shop. We need a drink.

JULIE Amen to that.

GERRY Will it be open?

JULIE Twenty-four hour.

Exit **GERRY** *outside.*

JULIE *inspects the carpet where he has been cleaning, she pokes through his kit.*

The doorbell rings. **JULIE** *opens it –.*

That was quick –

RUBY *pushes in. She has on the bloodied clothes and slippers we last saw her in. Her wrist is bandaged. She turns the lights off and ducks down below the windowsill.*

RUBY Is there a taxi outside?

JULIE What?

RUBY Look.

JULIE What's going on?

RUBY I had to do a runner at the lights at the bottom there. No cash, have I.

JULIE Have you discharged yourself?

RUBY I feel terrible.

JULIE I'm taking you back.

RUBY Not me. About the driver. He was telling me all about his two-legged cat. It's got wheels instead of back legs.

Anything?

JULIE No. Ruby –

RUBY I've never been in a taxi on my own before. I hailed it down in the street like I was in New York or something. Sticking to the seat cos the heater was blasting, the locks clicking, speeding through it all. People. Groups and pairs, on their own, talking, not, shrieking, smoking, waiting, leaving – *doing.*

JULIE They admitted you for a reason.

RUBY I feel fine. I feel…awake. The taxi driver was talking to me like I'm one of them, a real person. And I answered, chit-chat through the partition, giving him my address… Bollocks, I gave him my address.

A knock on the door.

Hide.

JULIE *opens the door. It is* **GERRY** *with a bottle.*

JULIE It's only Gerry.

GERRY There's a taxi here saying it needs paying?

JULIE Hang on.

JULIE retrieves her purse. Goes outside.

RUBY *(calling after her)* Tell him I'm sorry. And good luck with David Meowie.

GERRY Ruby.

RUBY Geraldine.

GERRY Julie said they were keeping you in.

RUBY Experience shows that hospitals like to remove things I get glass in. My eye, my foot and now my hand as well. A patch, a peg-leg and a hook would be taking the pirate look too far, even for me.

I'm joking. I'm being plucky.

Enter JULIE from outside.

JULIE All sorted.

GERRY I'll get that drink.

Exit GERRY to the kitchen.

RUBY I wasn't sure if you'd still be here.

JULIE Gerry's been doing his cleaning.

RUBY So I see.

Mam's still here.

JULIE Yeah.

RUBY I was thinking about it in the hospital.

JULIE Yeah?

RUBY It's a bit creepy, isn't it.

JULIE Yes.

Enter GERRY from the kitchen with a glass of wine. He sets it on the table.

GERRY The bottle's in the fridge.

JULIE Aren't you having one?

GERRY I'm going to shoot off. Early start.

You take care, Ruby.

RUBY *heads upstairs.*

JULIE Ruby?

RUBY I'm going for a piss, not to hang myself.

Exit **RUBY** *upstairs.*

JULIE I'm not going to tell her, if that's what you're doing.

GERRY It's up to you.

JULIE Gerry.

GERRY Yeah.

JULIE *(not cruel)* Don't ring me.

GERRY No?

JULIE I think we just… Ruby and I…

GERRY Ok.

He kisses her. She doesn't reciprocate, but nor does she stop him.

Exit **GERRY** *outside.*

After a time, **RUBY** *returns. She brings the bottle of lotion and some cotton wool pads.*

RUBY You don't realise how much you do with your left hand until you've sliced it to ribbons.

JULIE Does it hurt?

RUBY Yes.

JULIE I'm taking you back there first thing.

RUBY Ok.

Can you… my eye's flared up again and my hands aren't very steady.

JULIE lifts the eye patch and gently tends to RUBY's eye.

RUBY When I realised what I'd done…

I always thought, hoped…there was always tomorrow, you know. Tomorrow I'll do this, tomorrow I'll tell her I'd like to try that – but when I saw all the blood I was, like, fuck. I've done fuck all. And I've got fuck all to show for it.

JULIE You've got time. So much time.

RUBY Will you stay?

JULIE For a bit.

Silence. JULIE tends to her eye.

There's a full moon out there.

RUBY Are you going to turn into a werewolf?

JULIE We should bury the glass out the back. A full moon under a tree, wasn't it? Negates the bad luck.

RUBY Yeah.

JULIE We need all the help we can get.

RUBY And that. *(The jar)*

JULIE Yeah?

RUBY We should bury her out there too. I want to try without her watching.

Silence.

JULIE Ruby.

The beach. You said no-one saw you fall. How that made you feel.

RUBY I don't know what I was saying.

JULIE Yes you do.

RUBY It's when I became a totally new person. It just… I feel cheated that it could just happen in a flash, no-one looking.

JULIE I was looking.

RUBY No you weren't.

JULIE I was. I was there.

RUBY With Mam?

Ow.

JULIE *takes a moment.*

JULIE You were right about the sky falling in.

RUBY Was I?

JULIE Yes. Snow. Middle of summer, but the flakes were huge. Pure white drifting out of a clear blue sky, landing on you, disappearing into your clothes. Your face was turned away from me. Just hair. Each grain of sand around your head turned red. Sorry.

RUBY No, go on. All of it.

JULIE You didn't pull away. You were actually coming towards me. I was just an arm's reach away, but that distance was the world and my feet weren't moving. You sort of propelled forward. Your whole body in the air, like you were floating, like I might actually catch you. But I didn't. And I'm so sorry for that.

RUBY …

JULIE A man walking his dog ran up to one of the houses and called an ambulance.

RUBY …

JULIE *finishes with the lotion/pads.*

JULIE Done.

RUBY What kind of dog was it?

JULIE What?

RUBY Can you remember?

JULIE A sausage dog.

RUBY Cute.

RUBY *gets up and heads to the kitchen.*

Come on then. There's a spade in the shed you can use to dig the holes.

JULIE *gets up to follow.*

RUBY *turns and hugs* **JULIE**.

They stand there, in silence, for a time.

Eventually **RUBY** *breaks away. She exits to the kitchen.*

JULIE *composes herself and follows.*

The jar remains.

End

Act I
Property list

Dor keys (p1)
Bottoles on table (p2)
Mirror (p2)
Settee (p3)
Platter on coffee table (p4)
Glass of water (p2)
"Chicken fillets" from bra (p5)
Ugly support pants (p5)
Breakfast (p9)
Television and remote control (p9)
Glass of water (p9)
Bin bags (p10)
Julie's black dress (p11)
Plastic bag containing provisions (p12)
Cotton wool pads/lotion (p17)
Tea things and biscuits (p19)
Dirty plates and cups on the table (p23)
Post and junk mail lies on the mat (p23)
Plastic supermarket carrier bag (p23)
Squishy package (p25)
Brightly patterned cardigan (p25)
Bag (p27)
Bottle of tablets (p30)
Phone (p32)
The plated up meals are on the dinner table and a bottle of wine (p38)
Newspaper (p40)
Small pencil like the ones you steal from Ikea (p40)
Pair of reading glasses (p440)
Mini cheesecakes on a plate (p45)
Child's drawing (p49)
Parcel (p555)
Outer packaging reveals a cardboard box. She opens it and pulls out some packing foam (p56)
Glass jar – through cloudy liquid we can see there is an eyeball floating inside (p56)

Costume
Julie– smart black dress and heels (p1)
Gerry – smart too, but not a suit (p1)
Gerry – Coat (p5)
Ruby – dressing gown over pyjamas. Eye-patch (p7)
Gerry – same clothes from the night before (p12)
Julie – coat (p23)
Ruby – back of joggers are wet (p30)
Julie – wearing her new cardigan (p39)

Lighting

Room is in darkness (p1)
Julie turns the light on (p2)
Late afternoon (p23)
Curtains are drawn (p23)

Sound/Effects

Julie starts ringing on the doorbell (p6)
Julie leans on the bell – it rings unrelentingly (p6)
Telly is on – something loud and obnoxious (p9)
Julie finds the remote – reduces the volume (p9)
Turned the telly volume back up (p9)
Turns the telly back down (p9)
Ruby ups the telly volume louder still (p10)
Turns the telly off (p10)
Fumble of keys (p12)
The telly is on loud (p23)
We hear keys in the front door (P23)
Turns the telly off (p23)
Julie's phone beeps (p32)
Julie tries to take a mirror down….it drops and breaks (p55)

Act II
Property list

Empty frame of the broken mirror is propped against the wall (p59)
Gerry's camera bag (p59)
Two mugs of tea (p59)
Bloody tissues (p59)
Plastic carrier bag full of the broken mirror bits (p59)
Tiny shard of glass from the mirror (p59)
Camera (p60)
Cardboard box and thick manila envelope (p66)
Glass jar (p66)
Documents (p66)
Official looking letter (p70)
Mobile (p70)
Febreze (p70)
Printed out photo (p72)
Photo album (p72)
Sewing box (p72)
Button and a thread/needle (p72)
Handbag, phone, purse etc. (p75)
Cloth and bowl of water (p75)
Money (p75)
Freezer bag with a frozen eyeball inside (p77)
Shard of the mirror (p81)
Towel (p83)
Neat piles of paperwork (p86)
Photo album (p86)
Photo of Ruby (p87)
Suitcase (p88)
Fresh top (p89)
Purse (p95)
Glass of wine (p95)
Bottle of lotion and some cotton wool pads (p95)

Costume
Ruby – dressing gown. One of her feet has plasters on it (p659)

Gerry – dressed in a smart suit (p59)
Ruby – clean clothes, socks and slippers. Drying her damp hair with a towel (p70)
Julie – dressed in the same clothes as last time we saw her. She has slept in the (p74)
Julie – still has Ruby's dry blood on her clothes (p84)
Gerry – in his crime screen biohazard coverall and face-mask. He has his clean-up kit (p93)
Ruby – bloodied clothes and slippers we last saw her in. Her wrist is bandaged (p103)

Lighting

Very early hours of the following morning. It is still dark out. The lights are on (p84)
Turns the lights off (p93)

Sound/Effects

Doorbell rings (p73)
Gerry's phone rings (p76)
Keys in the front door (p84)
Doorbell rings (p93)
A knock on the door (p94)

Lightning Source UK Ltd.
Milton Keynes UK
UKOW06f0231050416

271558UK00001B/8/P